Bird-Watching Basics

FOR DUMMIES®

by Bill Thompson, III

D0896152

WILEY

Wiley Publishing, Inc.

Bird-Watching Basics For Dummies®
Published by
Wiley Publishing, Inc.
111 River St.
Hoboken, NJ 07030-5774
www.wiley.com

Copyright © 2006 by Wiley Publishing, Inc., Indianapolis, Indiana

Published by Wiley Publishing, Inc., Indianapolis, Indiana

WILEY

Publisher's Acknowledgments

We're proud of this book; please send us your comments through our Dummies online registration form located at www.dummies.com/register/. For information about a custom *Dummies* book for your business or organization, contact BrandedRights&Licenses@Wiley.com.

Some of the people who helped bring this book to market include the following:

Acquisitions, Editorial, and Media Development

Senior Project Editor: Zoë Wykes

Business Development Representative: Karen L. Hattan

Editorial Manager: Rev Mengle

Cover Photo: Leupold & Stevens

Composition Services

Project Coordinator: Kristie Rees

Layout and Graphics: Denny Hager, Stephanie D. Jumper, Heather Ryan, Brent Savage, Erin Zeltner

Proofreaders: Laura L. Bowman, Leeann Harney, Jessica Kramer

Indexer: Kevin Broccoli

Special Help
From Leupold & Stevens, Inc.:
Hilary Cosper, John Riutta

Publishing and Editorial for Consumer Dummies

    Diane Graves Steele, Vice President and Publisher, Consumer Dummies

    Joyce Pepple, Acquisitions Director, Consumer Dummies

    Kristin A. Cocks, Product Development Director, Consumer Dummies

    Michael Spring, Vice President and Publisher, Travel

    Kelly Regan, Editorial Director, Travel

Publishing for Technology Dummies

    Andy Cummings, Vice President and Publisher, Dummies Technology/General User

Composition Services

    Gerry Fahey, Vice President of Production Services

    Debbie Stailey, Director of Composition Services

Table of Contents

Introduction

*W*elcome to *Bird-Watching Basics For Dummies*. One of the many people who read an early draft of this book told me, "Reading this is just what it's like to go on a bird walk with you, Bill." That comment really pleased me because that's what I was after. You can write all you want about the subject of bird watching, but the very best thing to do, if you want to become a bird enthusiast, is to get outside and watch some birds. This book is designed to get you started in the right direction, and give you a sense of the fascination and joy that birds can bring to your life.

About This Book

I want this book, which was created specifically for the Leupold Bird-Watching Basics For Dummies Kit, to appeal to bird watchers, or birders, at every level of interest and expertise. But the majority of the information that I include is aimed at encouraging the beginner to take up the hobby of bird watching, and encouraging the intermediate bird watcher to explore the fringes of advanced birding. Advanced birders can find something of value in here, too, even if it's only that the text produces an occasional smile of recognition.

Think of this book as a reference. As such, it will serve you for the rest of your bird-watching days. You can come back to it time after time and search its pages for answers to your most nagging questions and for advice on getting better as a birder.

A few things about this book make it different from other books on bird watching, or *birding:*

- First, it's both fun to read and funny to read. I hope I give you a few laughs along the way.

- Second, it's written from my personal perspective (with some help from a few friends who also lent their perspectives) so you benefit from my own real-life experiences and mistakes, rather than from a generic editorial "we" voice.

✔ Third, this book is designed so that each chapter can stand alone content-wise, sort of like a giant buffet table of food. You can skip whole chapters that don't interest you at present, and read the juicy bits that seem appetizing. You can always come back later to sample the parts you skipped (but please remember to get a clean plate each time).

As you read through this book, you will notice the names of lots of different birds. I've chosen not to capitalize these names, except when they include a proper noun or name, such as Henslow's sparrow, as opposed to song sparrow. Although some bird folks claim that all bird names should be capitalized, I believe (and the rules of proper English language usage concur) that to "cap" all the first letters of every bird name is not only improper, it's overkill. I've tried to make it clear when I'm writing about the species yellow warbler, and a warbler that's colored yellow. I hope I've succeeded.

Why You Need This Book

When I was a young lad and just starting out as a bird watcher, I was fortunate to be able to follow in my mom's footsteps. I got to tag along with her bird club on outings and field trips, and, in doing so, I learned a lot about how to watch birds. If you don't know the basics of bird watching, you've come to the right place. I love teaching people about birds. One of my favorite things is to lead beginners on a bird walk.

Before I really found out how to be a bird watcher, I made all the rookie mistakes — not knowing how to focus binoculars properly, not knowing how to find the bird in the binoculars, not knowing where to find birds! Sometimes I was lucky if I could even find my binoculars! And I repeatedly made the classic beginner mistake of not taking my binoculars when my family went on a trip to another part of the continent. (How could I have thought that I wouldn't see many birds in Florida in winter!) If I'd only had a book like this. . . .

When you first venture out in search of birds to watch, you may have a frustrating experience. You may even have some of the beginner's misfortune I described. Don't worry! Bird watching or birding (I consider the terms interchangeable) is just like any other activity. The more you practice, the better you get. What's great about bird watching is that the practicing part is incredibly fun. The most important thing you can do to become a really good bird watcher is to relax and enjoy the birds you see. Without even trying to absorb information, you're gaining knowledge about the birds you watch simply by watching. How painless can it get?

When you positively identify your first bird species, all by yourself, and without lots of hints from a fellow birder, you realize the thrill of victory. It's that kind of experience that has kept me bird watching for all these years.

How to Use This Book

This book is designed to be read in pieces and parts (though if you decide to read it from cover to cover, that's fine too, and I'll be flattered).

I've included all kinds of information to help you become a better bird watcher, no matter where you are now, skillwise. If you become more interested in watching birds after reading this book, I've done my job.

How This Book Is Organized

This book is organized to help you ease into bird watching. The beginning bird watcher has a lot of questions, but may feel sheepish about asking these questions of another, more experienced bird watcher. That feeling of shyness is perfectly normal, and happens to almost everyone who takes up a new hobby or avocation. I can remember feeling that way for years until I felt confident enough to ask others questions. This book removes a lot of that awkwardness for you.

I've broken this book into eight chapters that cover everything from what exactly bird watching is to the tools that help you see and identify the birds, namely binoculars and a field guide. I also walk you through topics such as why birds do what they do (bird behavior and how to interpret it), and why birds make the sounds they do (bird songs, and how to recognize birds by their songs). I wish I had had such a good start when I was a young whippersnapper, just discovering birds! I even jump in and dispel many common myths about birds so as not to offend our fine feathered friends.

Icons Used in This Book

I guide you along on this birding trip with a series of icons. Think of them as roadside signs along the bird-watching highway. They alert you to upcoming tips, valuable advice, pitfalls, and even a few of my own bird-watching tales.

Marks things you can do to improve your birding and bird ID skills.

Identifies ways to make your backyard a paradise for birds.

Flags bird-watching terminology so you can chatter along.

Points out tips to improve your bird-watching skills wherever you are.

Highlights real stories about bird-watching life.

Watch out, but don't keep your head in the sand — pay attention or your birds may have flown.

Reminds you of important information to keep in mind.

Denotes ecologically sound practices that benefit birds, people, and other wildlife.

Chapter 1

Birds and the People Who Love Them

*D*o you ever look up, see a bird in flight, and find yourself wondering what kind of bird it is? You stare at it — noting its color, its shape, the spread of its wings. You watch it flit from branch to branch and fly away. And you wonder. Maybe you describe the bird to a family member or friend who may know what it is. Or you go to the library for a book about birds in the area to look up its picture. Or you wait, hoping to see it again just to appreciate the bird's beauty and song. That's bird watching. And you're already a bird watcher. Isn't that easy?

Today, bird watching (or birding) is a hobby enjoyed by millions and millions of people. Why? Because birds are fun to look at, birds are beautiful, many birds sing beautiful songs, and bird behavior is fascinating.

Wings and Feathers and Flight, Oh My!

A number of scientists now believe that birds may be living examples of the dinosaurs that once roamed the earth. One of the earliest-known birds is *Archaeopteryx,* discovered from fossilized remains found in Bavaria in 1851.

Archaeopteryx existed about 140 million years ago and had skeletal characteristics identical to those of small dinosaurs that lived during that same time. This creature also had a toothed jaw and feathers that allowed Archaeopteryx to glide from place to place (although its main mode of transport was likely clambering through branches).

Because of these features, some scientists believe that Archaeopteryx is one link between dinosaurs and what today we consider birds. Even though this creature didn't have the specialized bones and flight muscles that true birds have, Archaeopteryx is considered by many to be one branch of the evolutionary tree from which all birds may have descended. The link between Archaeopteryx and birds is a greatly debated subject that gets evolutionary scientists very worked up. I'll leave this one to the folks in the white lab coats. But one thing Archaeopteryx and birds have in common that seems to give them kinship is feathers, because, at its most basic, a bird is a creature that has feathers (see Figure 1-1) — the only type of creature that has feathers.

These feathers — along with lightweight, air-filled bones acquired through evolution — allow most birds to fly. Feathers are really highly evolved scales, like those found on reptiles such as snakes and lizards. (You can see the remnants of their reptilian ancestry on most birds' scaly legs and feet.) Besides promoting flight, feathers (also called plumage) regulate birds' temperatures and provide physical protection while giving birds their shape and color.

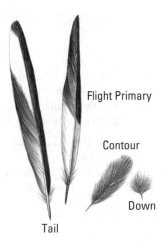

Flight Primary

Contour

Down

Tail

Figure 1-1: Feathers of a northern mockingbird — if it ain't got feathers, it's not a bird.

Here's a bonus obscure fact for you: A small songbird has more than 1,000 feathers on its body. A large swan, plucked by some patient soul, was found to have more than 25,000 feathers. Figure 1-2 shows a mute swan ruffling some of its 25,000 feathers.

Figure 1-2: Feathers help keep birds, such as this mute swan, comfortable, mobile, and beautiful.

Families and species

Without getting too technical, you need to understand two terms that bird watchers use a lot when referring to birds: *family* and *species*. Although I'm sure my ornithology professor will cringe (he always did anyway, which is probably why

I got a C!), here are *For Dummies*-approved definitions for the two terms:

- ✔ A *species* of birds is defined as a group of individuals that have similar appearance, similar behavior, and similar vocalizations, and that interbreed freely to produce fertile (able to breed successfully) young. When you identify a bird, you determine what species it is.

- ✔ A *family* of birds is made up of species that are very similar, but don't interbreed. You can find a more scientific definition of a bird family, but most bird watchers use this term to mean a group of birds that look, sound, and act in a similar way. For example, there are lots of different sparrow *species,* most of which belong to the sparrow *family.*

Remember both terms handily because you often hear them used when bird watchers try to identify a bird. If you see a small bird zipping through your flower garden, you may know to what family it belongs (hummingbird). Later, when you get a good look at the bird, you can identify its species (ruby-throated hummingbird).

Each species of bird has two types of names: a common name and a Latin name.

- ✔ The common name of a bird is the one that you're most likely to know. Common names, such as American robin, are the currency of bird watching.

- ✔ The Latin or scientific name, *Turdus migratorius* in the case of the American robin, is made up of two parts: the genus *(Turdus)* and the species *(migratorius).* Genus and species are two parts of the scientific classification system used to name all living creatures. Think of them as you would the first and last names of a person. Latin names are used to clarify the classification of birds and to help bird watchers and ornithologists (bird scientists) avoid confusion over regional and international differences in bird names. Just because they're Latin, don't let them scare you off. You won't be getting a pop quiz! And most bird watchers you encounter won't be fluent in the Latin names of birds, so you needn't be, either.

The number-one spectator sport

Today, an estimated 80 million people of all ages and physical abilities point their binoculars toward feathered creatures. Bird watching is second only to gardening as a favorite leisure time activity among North Americans. What's more, bird watching is considered the number-one spectator sport in North America!

Most of these 80 million people are watching the birds that come to their backyard feeders, but an increasing number of bird enthusiasts are venturing beyond their backyards to find more and different birds. And non-bird watchers are noticing. The average active bird watcher is estimated to spend more than $1,000 annually in pursuit of this hobby. I'm no good at math, but $1,000 x 80 million bird watchers is a lot of moolah. We bird watchers pack a significant economic wallop.

Bird watchers of a feather . . .

Bird watchers come in many types, from casual backyard looker to rabid, globe-trotting birder, and everything in between. I'm guessing that you're somewhere in between. Perhaps you already feed birds, and maybe you already own a pair of binoculars, but you don't yet consider yourself a bird watcher. Well, you've come to the right book.

Because you're reading this hypnotic prose of mine, you're already indicating an interest in the subject matter. What's great about bird watching is that you can enjoy it almost any-where, at any time, and at any level of involvement — always at your own pace.

Most folks who get into bird watching start by seeing birds in their backyard. Or perhaps somebody tugged their arms until they took hold of the binoculars being offered and looked at — oh my gosh! — a beautiful bird! What is it? Next comes getting a bird book, borrowing a pair of binoculars, and going out on their own to see birds. Soon they find a nearby bird club, join, and take some local bird trips. Maybe later they decide to go on a field trip to Florida or Texas with the club. At each point, more birds are seen and more friends made. Bird watchers can evolve much as birds have evolved.

Long gone are the days when the stereotypical bird watcher was a little old lady in tennis shoes or an absent-minded professor in a pith helmet (though these folks still exist). In those happily forgotten times, bird watchers were often the object of ridicule. The nerdy spinster character portrayed in *The Beverly Hillbillies* probably set bird watching back several decades as a socially acceptable activity.

If you find yourself wondering what your neighbors, co-workers, or friends will think, consider this: When you show an interest in birds, chances are, more than one of those folks will say, "I never knew you were a bird watcher! I love watching birds!"

Meeting your spark bird

For every bird watcher and birder, there's one bird that provided the catalyst, set the hook, was a spark (choose your metaphor) to begin that person's interest in birds.

For me, the spark bird was relatively nondescript, the American coot. Here's how it happened: I was sprung from school on a spring Friday and was allowed to accompany the local ladies' bird-watching club, of which my mom was a member. Because I wasn't interested in the birds they sought, I ran down the dirt road in the area where we were birding to see how many rocks I could throw off the bridge into Rainbow Creek. Just as I raised the first projectile into the air, I noticed something moving below. It was some kind of bird — perhaps a duck. I knew the gals up the road had yet to see a duck that day, so I ran to tell them of the sighting. They were incredibly thrilled! Coots in spring were not that common then in southeastern Ohio. I was surprised and a little embarrassed by the profuse shower of praise from the women. Soon they had me drumming up all sorts of birds. I was proud to point out birds to them. The following month, when I got a Friday off for another bird-watching trip, I didn't throw a single rock. I was hooked on birds.

A spark bird for you may be the scarlet tanager that your high school science teacher pointed out, or the red-tailed hawk shown to you by a scout leader. Better yet, it may be the singing male warbler you found yourself. Because you're reading this book, you may have found your spark bird already. If not, I envy you because finding the spark bird is a wonderful experience, and the start of a great adventure.

What makes a good bird watcher?

Two ingredients that a successful bird watcher has are a natural curiosity about the world and a healthy dose of enthusiasm. Both of these are invaluable. Why?

The natural curiosity leads you to do things you'd never do otherwise, such as get up at dawn on a beautiful May morning to hear the birds start singing. And the healthy dose of enthusiasm keeps you going on all those days when you've got more thumbs than there are birds to see. In that case, you make the most of the birds you *can* see.

Both of these admirable traits are great ones to pass along to friends who are beginners. It's the natural legacy and responsibility of all birders to pass the torch to those who come later. Return the favor to a beginner, just as you were guided by someone else.

Where the Birds Are

Birds are found almost everywhere. You'll read this statement repeatedly in this book. And here's another gem that bears repeating: Birds have wings and they tend to use them.

What these statements mean is that anywhere you're likely to be (outdoors, of course) you encounter birds. Going to the Arctic Circle on New Year's Day? Keep an eye out for snowy owls and snow buntings. Going to Antarctica for the Fourth of July? You'll be seeing penguins and other seabirds. Better have your binocs handy. Stepping out your backdoor to get some fresh air? No matter where you live, birds will be there, too.

The point is that you can be watching birds anytime and anywhere. After you get the hang of it, you'll be doing exactly that.

Chapter 2

Optics and How to Use Them

● ●

In This Chapter

▶ Optics defined

▶ What they do

▶ Starting out

▶ Choosing binocs

▶ Using binocs

▶ Avoiding a pain in the neck

▶ Trouble in paradise

▶ Cleaning and caring

● ●

*T*he binocular is the tool of the bird-watching trade. You can watch birds without the magnifying power of binoculars, but you won't always get a satisfactory look at the birds.

A myth about binoculars is that they're expensive. They can be, but they don't have to be. Recent advances in lens technology and the manufacturing process have resulted in very affordable binoculars for bird watchers.

In this chapter, I discuss what binoculars are, how they work, and how to choose them and use them most effectively for watching birds. Plus, I offer some tips on cleaning and loving your binoculars, because if you have decent binoculars, you *will* learn to love them, especially if they show you lots of neat birds.

Optics Defined: What You See Is What You Get

When birders talk about their optics, they're referring to their binoculars or spotting scope. Because the vast majority of the bird-watching public has binoculars (a.k.a. *binocs,* or *bins*), this is usually what is meant by the term *optics.*

Spotting scopes — higher-powered, single-tube (telescope) viewing devices — are used primarily for viewing distant birds, such as waterfowl or shorebirds. These high-powered scopes are becoming more popular as the number of avid bird watchers grows. But almost no one starts out with just a spotting scope — while everyone starts out with binocs of some sort. *Binoculars* are composed of two optical tubes, joined side by side, much like two miniature telescopes. Inside each tube is a series of lenses and prisms that reflect, magnify, and transmit light (see Figure 2-1). When binoculars are held up to your eyes and pointed at a distant object, a magnified image of that object is transmitted to your eyes — it looks bigger and closer than if you had no binoculars.

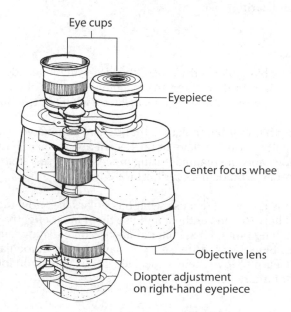

Eye cups

Eyepiece

Center focus whee

Objective lens

Diopter adjustment on right-hand eyepiece

Figure 2-1: A diagram of key parts of binoculars.

Two basic types of binoculars are used by modern bird watchers: Porro prisms and roof prisms. You can tell them apart by how they're constructed.

Porro-prism binocs

Porro-prism binoculars were first designed in the mid-1800s by some Italian fellow named Porro. His concept of placing two right-angled prisms in each barrel of a set of binoculars is still used today. Porro-prism binocs are commonly the stereotypical angled-body binocular design; however, modern versions can also be Inverted Porro, like the Leupold 8x25mm binoculars in this kit. When standing on their barrels, or hanging from a strap around someone's neck, Porro-prism binoculars appear to form an M shape (see Figure 2-2); Inverted Porroprism models form a W shape.

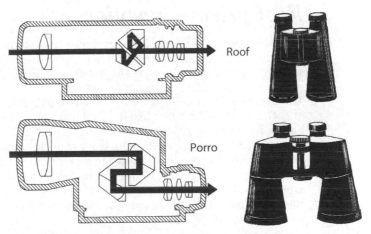

Figure 2-2: How roof (top) and Porro-prism binoculars work.

Porros focus by relying upon an external focus wheel that, when turned, causes specific lenses in each side of the binoculars to move along a controlled pathway. This type of focusing allows for sharp, 3D images of birds and other objects. Inverted Porro-prism models excel at precise focusing on objects as close as 6 to 10 feet.

The advantages of this binocular design are

- ✔ Brighter images due to greater transmission of light
- ✔ Fast focusing
- ✔ Close focusing (Inverted Porro models)
- ✔ Wide field of view (the amount of area you see when looking through the binoculars)

For low-to-mid-range priced binoculars, Porro- and Inverted Porro-prisms offer the best value.

The disadvantages are weight (the better transmission of light is due to large prisms, which are weighty) and bulkiness, which can make Porros hard to use for small-handed folks. (Inverted Porro-prism models eliminate these disadvantages.)

Roof-prism binoculars

Roof-prism binoculars were first developed by a German fellow named Hensold in the late-1800s. This design features two straight barrels, giving it an H-shaped appearance.

The design gets its name from the shape of one of the prisms in each barrel — they look like the roof of a house. Roof-prism binocs have grown in popularity among birders in the last few decades, primarily because many leading optics manufacturers are producing excellent optics in this format for the bird-watching market. Because of the way roof-prisms are designed, most of the focusing hardware is enclosed inside the body of the binoculars. This hardware is adjusted with an external focusing knob or wheel.

The advantages to roof-prism binoculars are

- ✔ Ease of handling
- ✔ Fewer external moving parts
- ✔ A better ratio of power-to-weight; that is, in general, a 10x roof-prism weighs less than a 10x Porro
- ✔ Excellent potential for close focus distances of less than 10 feet

At the mid-to-high-range price for binoculars, roof-prisms dominate the market.

The disadvantages are that roof-prisms tend to be more expensive than Porros. Because of the additional prism complexity required to reflect incoming light, specific low-quality roof-prism models often do not offer as "bright" or "sharp" an image as Porros.

Choosing Binoculars

You need to consider a number of factors when choosing binoculars, but the most important three are *quality, power* (or magnification), and *comfort*. When selecting binoculars for yourself, bear these three factors in mind. Neglect any one of them, and you'll almost certainly regret your decision later.

For example, if you decide to buy a lower-quality binocular even though you like a higher-quality, more pricey pair better, you may find at a later date that you wished you'd made the additional investment. Or if you purchase a large pair of bins that seem too large in your hands just because the clerk says "They're the best!" you'll regret it later in the field. Like shoes, binoculars should fit right from the beginning.

Before you buy, I suggest you gather all the information you can about binoculars. Ask your friends and fellow birders about their binocs. What brand and power do they have? What do they like about them? What do they dislike? How much did they pay? Where did they buy them? Would they do anything differently the next time they buy binoculars? What is the warranty? Are the binoculars waterproof? If you can get answers to these questions, you'll begin to get a picture of what *you* would prefer in binoculars.

Binoculars need to feel comfortable to you. Never buy for a brand name alone — always make your comfort and ease of use the primary point of choice, and balance it with all your other gathered information.

Power

The best binoculars for bird watching come in the 6x to 10x range (that's 6-power to 10-power). Binocs in this range provide enough magnification to make distant birds look bigger, without being too heavy to hold steady or to have hanging around your neck.

Be careful with 10x as it can be too powerful for some people and some situations.

Power is as much a matter of personal preference as anything. You may like the high magnification of 10x binoculars, but their increased weight may make your arms tired after holding them to your eyes for only a few minutes. Try several different binocs, either at a camera/optics store or at a gathering of bird watchers. You'll notice a difference in weight between binocs of different powers. Any binoculars above 10-power are likely to be too heavy to hold still, but can be used successfully when mounted on a tripod.

Binocular terms

These terms are helpful to know if you wish to be fluent in binocular-speak:

✔ **Armoring:** An outer coating, often rubber or synthetic, that makes binoculars more durable and easier to hold.

✔ **Close focus:** How closely a pair of binoculars can focus (under 12 feet is ideal for most birders). Many high-power binoculars can't focus on objects that are nearer than 20 feet. This limitation is a disadvantage for birders wishing to look at nearby birds or butterflies. To determine the close focus of a binocular, try to focus on your feet, or another nearby object. The distance to the closest object upon which you can focus clearly is the close focus value of your binocular.

✔ **Eye relief:** The distance from your eyes to the outer surfaces of the eyepiece lenses. You don't want your eyes or eyelashes to touch the lenses, but if the eye-relief distance is too short or too great, you

lose field of view. Imagine peeking through a hole in a fence: The closer your eye gets to the hole, the more area you can see through the hole.

✔ **Eyepiece:** The lens nearest your eyes (the end of the binoculars that you look into).

✔ **Field of view:** The amount of area that can be seen when looking through a pair of binoculars. A larger field of view makes finding a distant bird through your binoculars easier. A good rule to follow is the lower the magnification, the greater the field of view, that is, higher powered binocs (10x and up) often have substantially narrow fields of view compared to 8x or especially 6x models.

✔ **Lens coatings:** Treatments applied to binocular lenses to increase image clarity, brightness, and color quality. Coated lenses are one of the things that make expensive binoculars expensive, but also better.

> ✔ **Objective lens:** The lens nearest the object at which you're looking. The diameter of the objective lens, measured in millimeters, is the second number in the two numbers used to describe optics.
>
> ✔ **Power:** The amount of magnification provided by the binoculars. Usually listed as 7x, 8x, or 10x.
>
> ✔ **6x30, 8x25, 8x42:** Pronounced "6 by 30," and so on. The common model designation for binoculars. The first number is the power or magnification (a 6x or 6-power binocular magnifies a distant bird six times, making it appear six times closer). The second number indicates the size of the objective lens (the larger end, not the one you look through). The larger this number, the larger the objective lens. (A common mistake is to assume that a large objective lens means a large field of view. This idea is wholly incorrect as the objective lens has next to nothing to do with the field of view.)

Recent advances in binocular design have helped make binoculars lighter and better balanced in the hand. The mantra is "Try before you buy!"

Using the logic that more is better, wouldn't a 12x50 binocular be great? Lots of magnification and lots of light? The answer is an emphatic *no!* Such powerful binocs require large lenses and internal prisms, which make them almost impossibly heavy to use without mounting them on a tripod.

Never look directly at the sun through binoculars. Magnified sunlight can seriously damage your eyes. When bird watching, always be aware of the sun's position so you don't inadvertently point at or swing your binocs past the sun. Ouch!

Comfort

"The best binoculars," an optics expert once wrote, "will disappear from your awareness while you are using them."

When you try binoculars, ask yourself if they feel comfortable to use. Comfort is a combination of factors: Are they easy to raise to your eyes? Does your forefinger automatically rest on the focus wheel? Can you easily adjust the settings to fit your needs? Do the binocs feel very heavy around your neck? Do they feel good in your hands?

You can have the best optics money can buy, but if you're not comfortable using them, they may as well be a lead doorstop. Here's an analogy for you: I'd love to own a racy sports car. There's one problem though (besides lack of money): I am 6'4" tall, and there's no way I can fit into a sports car. Sexy and stylish though it may be, I am miserably uncomfortable in a tiny car.

If you have trouble holding a pair of binoculars steady (if the image is constantly moving and jiggling), the binocs may be too heavy or of too high a power for you to use. Try using a friend's lighter or smaller binoculars and see if you have a more stable image.

Other considerations

If I haven't confused you yet about how to choose binoculars, here are some other things to think about.

Field of view

Make sure the binoculars you choose have a reasonable field of view (the amount of area you can see at one time when looking through the binocs). Binoculars with narrow fields of view make it hard to find the bird when you raise the optics to your eyes. A good field of view is at least 6° for an 8x model or at least 7.5° for a 6x model.

Close focus

An ideal pair of binoculars focuses on objects as close as 12 feet away. Some models focus on closer objects. High-powered binocs, such as my own 10x4z wonders, may only focus to about 20 feet. This limited focus is a drag when a warbler perches 10 feet away and I have to *naked-eye* it while my wife *oohs* and *ahhs* at the close look she can get through her 8-powers.

Brightness

The level of image brightness produced by your binoculars is a factor of the optical design, how large the objective lenses are (x35, x40, x42, and so on), and the quality and coatings of the optical elements (lenses and prisms).

Lens coatings

Coated lenses and high-quality prisms reduce the amount of light lost, and thus transmit more light, which makes a brighter image. Test several models with coated and uncoated optics and you can see the difference. But remember, the better the coatings, the more expensive the binoculars are likely to be.

Armoring/waterproofing

If my binoculars weren't armored, I'd have smashed and dented them at least 400 times since I got them ten years ago. Armoring is a rubberized coating that encases the binoculars (but not the lenses), providing protection from bumps and knocks. Quality field-use binocs should always be water*proof,* not just water *resistant.*

Be careful of zoom binoculars, not to be confused with dual-magnification binoculars, which *may* have inferior optics to regular non-zoom models (there are good ones out there but they don't come cheap). Avoid fixed-focus field glasses, which are simply impractical for watching birds. Avoid binoc-ulars that lack a center focus wheel — meaning they can *only* be focused by turning the two individual eyepieces. These binocs are too hard to use in the field, if you only have two hands.

Using Binoculars

For several years after I started watching birds, I didn't know how to focus my binoculars properly. I'm going to save you from a fate such as mine (and save you from some painful headaches). When a friend finally showed me how to *really* focus binoculars, I couldn't believe how 3D the birds looked all of a sudden! And I had no moment of dizziness after lower-ing my binocs. My next move was to beg my parents for new and better binoculars.

Using binocs isn't as simple as raising them up to your eyes. But the process is pretty simple nonetheless. Because not all eyes are created equal, binoculars are designed to be adjusted to accommodate your needs.

Setting the eyespace

All good binoculars are made in a way that allows the two optical barrels to pivot so that the space between them can be adjusted. When using binoculars, it's key that you get the two halves of the binocs the right distance apart to get the maximum image size. This spacing should match the amount of space between your eyes' pupils (called *interpupillary distance*).

That statement may seem overly obvious to you, but you'd be surprised how many bird watchers use binocs for years without getting the eyespace aligned properly for their eyes. (If you've ever appeared in a Picasso painting and both of your eyes are on the same side of your nose, please ignore this section.)

To set the eyespace of your binoculars correctly, push the two barrels together so that they're adjusted to their minimum spacing. Raise the optics to your eyes and slowly expand the space between the barrels until you have the maximum amount of view or image space. If the barrels are too close together, the image area you see is circular and you may be able to see your hands or lots of black space out of the corners of your eyes. If the barrels are too far apart, you see two separate image circles with a black area in between.

If you have the proper eyespace for your eyes, your image area appears oval-shaped and you notice the large, clear image space.

If you wear glasses, always twist or fold the eyecups all the way down to the binocular itself so that the lens of your eyeglasses can be as close as possible to the eyepiece lens of the binocular. Otherwise, the eyecup will greatly reduce your field of view because your eye is farther away from the eyepiece lens than is ideal. Think of it this way: Isn't it easier to see more through a keyhole if your eye is right up next to the hole?

Using the diopter: The eye equalizer

Almost everyone has one eye that is stronger than the other. This means that when the eyes focus on a distant object, the images transmitted to your brain from each eye are different. In addition, many people suffer from near-sightedness or far-sightedness. If your eyes aren't a perfectly matched 20-20, you may have a difficult time using binoculars because you can't focus clearly.

The word *diopter* is used by optometrists to measure the amount of correction needed for eyeglass prescriptions. The diopter (sometimes spelled dioptre) adjustment on binoculars compensates for these differences between eyes, as well as for any near-sightedness or far-sightedness. Adjusted properly, the diopter helps you to focus clearly on your target image.

You can use two basic configurations for adjusting a diopter. One is controlling the diopter adjustment with a second focus wheel, most commonly mounted in front of the right eyepiece (refer to Figure 2-1) of the binoculars. Once set, these markings, with 0 as a center point, allow you to remember the best setting for your eyes.

Using a diopter is an intrinsic part of focusing your binoculars.

Focusing

To focus your binoculars properly, follow these easy steps:

1. **Adjust the eyecups by twisting them up or down so that you see a full image in each eyepiece lens (if you wear eyeglasses and wish to use them with the binoculars, be sure that the eyecups are all the way down so that the eyepiece lens is nearly flush with the edge of the eyecup).**

2. **Adjust the binoculars so that the eyepieces are the right distance apart for your eyes.**

   You should see a single image when using both eyes.

3. **Choose a stationary object at a moderate distance on which to focus.**

4. **Looking through the binoculars, cover the right** *objective lens* **(the end farthest away from you when looking through the binoculars), and using the** *focus dial* **(the big dial in the center), focus the binoculars on your chosen object.**

5. **Cover the left objective lens and, without touching the focus dial, use the** *diopter control dial* **(located just below the right eyepiece), turning it until the object is in focus for your right eye.**

6. **Finally, check the image seen through the binoculars with both eyes.**

   The image should be balanced and equally clear. If not, go back to Step 3 and try it again.

   When you get the focus just right, the image you see "feels" right to you. It almost looks like a three-dimensional image, and your eyes won't be straining to resolve the image; they'll feel relaxed.

7. **Look at the symbols or numbers on the right eyepiece or secondary focus knob; note where your focus point is and remember it.**

   Next time you pick up your binocs (especially after someone else has used them), you can automatically adjust the focus setting to this position.

After you get your binocs focused and the diopter adjusted for your own eyes, the only focusing you have to do is with the center focus wheel. Properly focused, your binoculars give you a crystal-clear image. When I discovered this, the birds seemed clear and sharply defined to my eyes for the first time.

You can get fast at focusing by practicing on stationary objects. To set my binocs, I always pick an object with lots of contrast, such as a dark tree branch against a light sky or a black-and-white highway sign or billboard. Before long, focusing becomes second nature to you.

Trouble in Paradise: Balky Bins

If you're new to this binocular-toting hobby called bird watching, you may be having some less-than-heavenly experiences using your optics. This is normal, even for veteran bird watchers! The happy news is that all these problems are easy to remedy.

Focus problems

If you can't seem to get your birds in focus, even after following the steps in the section on "Focusing," earlier in this chapter, here are two suggestions:

- ✔ Clean your binoculars thoroughly and try again.

- ✔ Take or send your binoculars to the manufacturer and ask that the alignment be checked.

Binoculars can go out of alignment from a hard bump or knock, just like the tires on your car. Out-of-alignment binocs are impossible to focus precisely, so your eyes try to adjust to make up for the lack of focus. The result is headache, dizziness, and frustration for you.

To find a person trained to fix optics, call or e-mail your binoculars' manufacturer, ask the company that sold you the optics, or inquire at your local camera store.

Dizzy eyes

If your binoculars are not truly in focus, or if they're out of alignment, you may experience a moment of dizziness after you lower the binocs from your eyes. Believe me, it's better to solve this problem than to continue to use the binocs as they are. If you can't eliminate the problem by refocusing, or by using your diopter adjustment, call the manufacturer of your binoculars and inquire about their repair service.

Glasses

If you wear eyeglasses, you don't have to suffer through reduction of image space or field of view because your glasses prevent your eyes from getting as close as possible to the eyepieces of the binoculars. Today, most quality binoculars feature eyecups that improve comfort for users, whether bespectacled or not. For the glasses-wearer, these eyecups can be twisted (or rolled) down, allowing you to place the binoculars up against your glasses. This permits your eyes to be as close as possible to the outer lens of the eyepiece, which gives you an enlarged field of view. It also prevents the binoculars from scratching your glasses. Avoid older (and cheapo) binoculars that have metal eyecups.

With a little practice, you can raise your binocs to your glasses without jamming your glasses into your nose. Always make sure the eyecups are squared-up with your glasses, so that you're not cheating yourself out of the largest possible field of view. You may find that it helps to have a second pair of glasses, specifically for bird watching. Find a pair that allows you to get as close as possible to your binoculars' eyepieces. If your regular glasses are bifocals, ask your optician to move the bifocal line as low as possible on your glasses' lenses. This step makes using your binocs easier.

If you don't wear glasses, extend the eyecups to help block side light from entering your view.

Warbler neck

Warbler neck can happen with or without binoculars. It's caused by looking up for long periods, perhaps at some treetop warblers or soaring hawks. To avoid it, stretch out on the ground. This way you can scan the skies while your aching neck gets a rest.

Can't find the bird

You set your sights on the bird and you can't find it. This is by far the most commonly made rookie mistake. You see a bird. You lift your binoculars to your eyes. You start moving your head around crazily looking for the bird. Relax, will ya?

Here's a trick. See a bird. Note where the bird is in relation to a nearby (to the bird) landmark, such as a red leaf, a crooked branch, a clod of dirt, or whatever. LOCK YOUR EYES ON THE BIRD AND DON'T MOVE THEM! Bring your binocs up to where your eyes are. Line up the binocs on the landmark that you spotted, and the bird should be easy to find — unless the bird has flown.

Fogging

There are certain times when you just have to put up with your bins fogging up, such as when you walk into a warm house after being outside in very cold weather. This is external fogging and will go away in a few minutes. If your binocs fog up on the inside, you need to seek professional help (for them). Good binoculars don't fog internally. If they do, some moisture is inside them, which is not good. Get them looked at by the manufacturer or by an authorized repair person.

How to Carry Your Bins

Strap it up, I'll take it! *Always, always, always* use some kind of strap or harness with your binoculars. If you don't — mark my words — you'll be sorry. And even if you do have a strap on your bins, but you tend to get lazy and hand carry them by the strap, beware! You will drop them at some point.

Now that I have all that gloom and doom out of my system, let me mention that you should have a strap for your binoculars and you should wear it around your neck. A strap is not just a convenient, hands-free way of carrying your optics, it's also a kind of safety belt for them.

A good neckstrap is soft, hooks securely to your binoculars, adjusts to fit your length preference, and feels comfortable holding *your* binoculars around *your* neck.

Many straps included with binoculars are just fine. Excellent straps and harnesses that fit any model of binocs are available by mail order or in any store that sells cameras. If you plan to do a lot of birding, invest in a strap that is comfortable for you.

A variation on the around-the-neck theme is the binocular harness. These units *really* spread out the weight of your optics by means a of criss-crossing shoulder harness. Though they take some getting used to, they are often worth it. I know several harness users (myself included) who claim to have been free of neck and back problems since adopting one of these alternative straps.

When watching birds from a car that has automatic shoulder seatbelts — the kind that slide automatically into place whenever the car is started or the door is shut — be careful of where your binoculars are. If you're behind the seatbelt strap, but your binoculars and strap are in front, watch out when the strangulation device — I mean the seatbelt — begins its unmerciful trip to its destination. You can find your neck in the most uncomfortable viselike grip of an object intended to save your life.

Always pull over and stop before glassing a bird.

If your binoculars bounce around and pound against your chest or stomach when you walk, here are three solutions:

✔ Change the way you walk, or quit birding from a pogo stick. If this isn't practical . . .

✔ Shorten your binocular strap; most straps have a slip-through buckle for making this adjustment on either end, near where they connect to the binoculars. Or . . .

✔ Purchase one of the harness-type straps that holds your optics snugly against your body. The added benefit is that a good harness distributes the weight evenly across your back and shoulders.

Cleaning and Caring

Clean binoculars are happy binoculars. If your binocs are like mine, you can practically recall every meal you've ever eaten over them. The hard-to-reach areas around the lenses hold a veritable food-museum's worth of crumbs and UFO's (unidentifiable foodlike objects). There's no time like the present to clean up your act.

Spotting scopes

For 85 percent of the bird watching you do, your binoculars likely give you adequate performance in magnification and image clarity. However, for some birding situations where the birds are quite distant, you can enjoy better looks at birds by using a spotting scope. A spotting scope is one optical tube (binoculars have two) that generally offers greater magnification (above 20 power) than binoculars (usually between 6 and 10 power).

Here's how:

1. Get lens-cleaning fluid and a lens cloth from a drugstore, camera store or eye-doctor's office.

2. Blow forcefully on each lens to loosen bits of dirt, bread crumbs, or hardened mayonnaise.

3. Using a crumpled lens cloth or soft-bristled brush, brush lightly across each lens.

4. Wet a clean lens cloth with lens cleaning fluid and lightly wipe each lens in a circular motion, starting in the center of each lens and moving progressively outward.

5. Use a clean and dry lens cloth to wipe excess moisture from the lenses, starting in the center of each lens and moving progressively outward.

For heavily mayo-covered lenses, two rounds of cleaning may be in order.

To clean the body of your binoculars, which may be coated in french-fry grease, dampen a cloth with water and wipe.

Don't wipe your binocular lenses with your shirt tail. Take the time to clean them properly and they'll pay you back with great vision for years to come. Take the sloppy way out and wipe them with your sleeve and you'll put thousands of tiny, light-bending scratches on the lenses. This type of behavior puts you on the road to binocular ruin. Breathing on the lenses and then rubbing them with your shirt tail or a facial tissue is also not good. Only resort to such "seat of the pants" cleaning methods in an emergency.

Chapter 3

Tools That Take You Up Close and Personal

● ●

● ●

*A*s a bird watcher, you need very little in the way of gear or stuff in order to enjoy bird watching. In fact, I recommend only two primary tools that are essential to getting the most out of this sport: *binoculars* and a *field guide* to the birds.

The only other thing that you need is a place to watch birds, and that can be almost anyplace. Birds are among the planet's most common and widespread creatures. Walk out your front door, drive to work, and look out the window — you've probably had bird accompaniments the whole trip. You see birds almost everywhere.

The Optics Option

Okay. If you see birds everywhere, why do you need binoculars or other optical help?

Well, let me clarify one thing about optics: You *don't* need to have binoculars and other optics to watch birds. If you're satisfied and utterly fulfilled by looking at a bird in a tree 50 yards away and saying to yourself, "Hey, there's a bird!" you don't need optics. But if you're like most members of our species (upright-walking, thumb-using, living indoors, . . .), you'll want to *identify* that bird. Is it a sparrow or a finch? Or just a blurry-yellow-thingie-with-wings? How will you know if you see it again?

Binoculars let you get a closer look, which lets you see clues to the bird's identity. With these clues (and a field guide!), you can solve the mystery of just about any bird's identity.

I don't want to show disrespect to the millions of people who are perfectly happy to see birds only at their backyard feeders. That's where most of us start out with birds. And the birds you invite for dinner can put on quite a show. But let's face it, even birds that appear at your feeders have names, and you won't know many of them without a good look at the bird and a corresponding look at a good field guide. And beyond your backyard is a whole world of amazing birds just waiting to introduce themselves when you get them in your sights. I guarantee that if you decide to become a bird watcher, you'll be much happier looking at birds through binoculars.

Bird watchers use many different terms for their binoculars. Two of the most common are *binocs* and *bins.* Generically, binoculars and the telescopes used for birding are called *optics,* which is easier to say than optical equipment. I also have heard bird watchers use some unprintable names for their binoculars, often after they missed seeing a bird because their binocs were fogged or of poor quality.

If you're just starting out, you've started in the right place. Unlike many beginners who start without binoculars, you have in this kit the Leupold 8x25mm binoculars (which are very good beginning binoculars) so you're already set to go. I started out with a pair of old Army binocs that my great aunt had in her attic (no, she wasn't in the Army). These old binocs were awful, but they gave me a better-than-naked-eye view of birds. After my folks saw my interest in birds, we got a family pair of binocs. These weren't much better, but at least they didn't have 100-year-old mayonnaise on the lenses.

Take the binocs outside and practice by looking at a distant stationary object. They should feel good in your hands, be easy to raise and lower, easy to focus, and they should not leave you with a dizzy feeling or a headache after you lower them from your eyes (this is eye strain caused by out-of-focus or poorly aligned binoculars, or because you haven't calibrated them to your vision yet).

Eventually, as your interest in bird watching grows, you may want to purchase a more advanced model of binoculars. The next level of quality in binoculars is the $100 to $300 range. You can get very nice binoculars in this range, especially at the upper end.

Your Field Guide

The second piece of very useful equipment for bird watching is a field guide to the birds. If you're a beginning bird watcher, the field guide can be a big help as you learn to identify birds.

A field guide is like a family album of birds, but even better. It contains color images of birds, maps showing where the birds can be found during certain seasons of the year, and descriptive text that covers information about the bird that can't be conveyed by either images or maps.

Remember those games you played as a kid where you matched the colors with the shapes? The purple square with the other purple square, and so on? Using a field guide to identify birds is just like that. You see a bird that you don't recognize; you make a mental note about its color, shape, and general appearance; and then you look for a matching bird image in the field guide.

Bird watching is the process of seeing and identifying birds. True, you don't have to identify each bird that you see. You don't even have to identify *any* of the birds that you see. But one of the most fun things about bird watching is solving the mystery of each bird's identity using the clues that I gather. Maybe I get a nice long look at a wading waterbird or a perched bird of prey, giving me plenty of time to gather identifying clues, or *field marks*. Or I may get a brief glimpse of a tiny warbler flitting through the treetops. In both cases, I take the clues and begin my detective work using a field guide.

A matter of choice

Depending on where in North America you live (or where on the planet you live), you can choose from several field guides.

- ✔ Some guides cover all the birds of North America (north of Mexico) in a single book; others divide the continent into East and West.

  Bird watchers in the eastern third of the continent can get by with just an eastern guide, and those in the western third can get by with a western field guide. But those folks in the middle third of the continent need to have access to information about all the birds, east and west.

- ✔ Specialty field guides are also available. Some cover all the birds of a given region, such as the Pacific Northwest, the Great Basin, Texas, Arizona, or Florida. Other guides are focused not upon geography, but upon families of birds, such as guides to the hawks of the world, warblers of the world, or ducks, geese, and swans of the world.

- ✔ Major, non-specialty field guides also have variation. Some use photographs to show you the birds, others use artwork. Some guides feature images, descriptive text, and species' range maps on the same page.

Some guides are better for beginners; others are better for more experienced bird watchers. As a beginner, you will do better with a field guide of a limited area. That way you won't need to wade through pages of birds that appear on the other side of the country to locate the bird you saw. The brochure of common feeder birds, included in this kit, is an ideal tool to use in identifying the most common birds that you will likely see in your own backyard.

Don't leave home without it

I know it seems like I'm trying to get you to spend all your money, but trust me: You *will* want more than one field guide.

I like keeping one in the car, one at the office (okay, I have dozens at the office), and several at home. Even though I've been bird watching for 35 years, I still prefer to have a field guide with me whenever I go out to watch birds. I may not carry it with me, and I may not even need to open it while I'm in the field; but when I need the guide, I *really* need it. You never know when something unfamiliar will turn up, or when the field guide will provide the clinching bit of information to solve the day's greatest bird identification mystery. You'll find, however, that as you get more familiar with bird identification, you'll refer to the field guide less and less.

Chapter 4

Identifying Birds ("If It Walks Like a Duck...")

- -

In This Chapter

▶ Parts is parts

▶ First impressions

▶ Field marks

▶ Bird behavior and other clues

▶ Field guide inspection

- -

*A*ll birds have an identity, also known as a species name (refer to Chapter 1). Central to the joy of watching birds is identifying those birds you see.

Bird identification is a matter of sifting through various clues to solve the mystery of a bird's identity. It's a process of elimination in which you eliminate all the birds that aren't the one you're looking for. Most of these clues — behavior, size, shape, color, habitat, and important field marks — are visual. Sound plays a role with some birds — bird song, wing whistle, and so on — but your eyes do most of the clue sifting. (I've yet to see a guide to birding by nose. Perhaps it's just a matter of time.)

The first time you try to identify a strange bird, you may be overwhelmed and confused by the possibilities. What seems like a perfectly obvious small brown bird sitting on your feeder leads to pages and pages of small brown birds to choose from in your field guide. Don't despair. Identifying birds *is* possible, and you don't have to be a genius or devote your life to the study of small brown birds.

Remember, everyone starts out knowing nothing. Millions of bird watchers have mastered the trick of casually throwing a name (sometimes the right one!) on the birds they see. Most of these watchers are no smarter than you. They all started out just like you — appreciating the beauty and wonder of birds and wanting to know more about them. This chapter takes you through the basic steps of identifying a bird.

Before long, that small brown bird at your feeder becomes a female house finch. See, you're learning already!

The Parts of a Bird

Knowing the parts of a bird is very helpful when it comes to bird identification. If you see a strange bird that has some yellow on it, this information is of no use unless you know *where* the yellow is on the bird. If you're new to bird watching, some of the bird parts may also be new to you.

Think chicken

Figure 4-1 shows some of the most common parts used by bird watchers to identify birds. Some parts have more specialized names that are used in bird identification.

If you've ever cooked, eaten, or looked at a chicken, you already know almost all the parts of a bird (see Figure 4-2). You don't need to be a bird watcher to know where the legs, breast, head, bill, wings, tail, and feet are. By the time you eliminate all the words and parts you already know, you're left with about half a dozen words that are unique to bird watching. Yes, these words may be unfamiliar, but everyone can remember at least six words. For most people, it takes about 15 minutes, the time you take to have that morning cup of coffee.

Take a few minutes to study the parts of a bird. Once you know what a *flank* and a *supercilium* (the area above the bird's eye) and a *wingbar* are, and say the words aloud, the terms lose their mystique and their ability to cloud your mind. Not only does the descriptive text in the field guide now make sense, but you can now toss these words casually into bird-watching conversations with others so that you sound like an expert, even if you still have trouble telling a bald eagle from an oven-ready roaster.

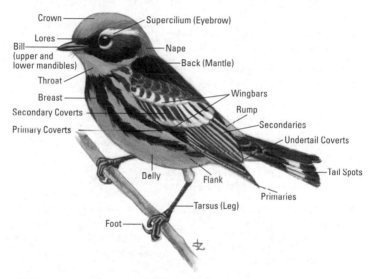

Figure 4-1: The parts of a bird as shown on a male magnolia warbler.

Figure 4-2: A robin and a chicken: kin under the skin.

Non-chicken bird parts defined

Eyeline: A line of contrasting color (usually black or white) that goes through or above the eye.

Eyering: A ring of color (usually white) that encircles the eye. A broken eyering is one that isn't continuous.

Wingbar: Contrasting stripes of color on the bird's wing in the shoulder area.

Rump patch: A patch of color above where the tail connects to the body.

Breast: Okay, chickens do have these. The area from below the bird's throat to the midway point on its lower body. The area below the breast is the belly.

Lores: Zone between the bird's eye and bill.

Supercilium: The area above the bird's eye, also called the eyebrow.

Flank: The area between the bird's side and tail.

Nape: The back of the bird's neck.

Mantle: Between the bird's wings, below the nape.

Mandible: The bird's bill comprises two parts, the upper mandible and the lower mandible.

Primary feathers: The longest of the wing feathers; the ones that form the pointed edge when the wing is folded.

Secondary feathers: The feathers that form the trailing edge along the middle of a bird's wing. The secondaries are the innermost flight feathers between the bird's body and its primary feathers.

Pay attention to field marks

Field marks are unique characteristics that separate one bird from another. Almost all birds have a distinctive set of field marks that make it possible to tell one species from another. Finding out how to identify a bird is understanding what its field marks are. In very few cases, the field marks are so subtle, they can't be seen in the field. Consider those birds a challenge to be tackled at a later date. A good pair of binoculars is indispensable in picking up the broadest range of field marks. As you progress, you find yourself automatically noticing the field marks of each bird you encounter, much as you would recognize a friend after a while. Here's something to get you started on the road to bird identification enlightenment.

Before you grab (or run out and buy) a field guide to the birds, take this simple test of your observation skills. This exercise calibrates your visual settings and helps you to look at each bird in an analytical way. You can do this exercise even if you don't have a field guide.

> ✔ Pick a common bird, one you can easily see in your area or yard, such as a cardinal, robin, or chickadee. Already knowing the species of the bird helps. For this example, I use the male cardinal (forgive me if you aren't familiar with this species). Every time I write *cardinal,* you just mentally fill in the blank with your choice of a familiar bird, okay?
>
> ✔ Look at the familiar bird and make written notes about its appearance. Note anything you feel may be a clue to its identity.

What you write probably looks something like this:

A bright red bird with a red point of feathers on its head. A black face. Average size, not small, but not huge. Hopping around beneath the bird feeder eating sunflower seeds. Chips loudly every so often.

Here's what a field guide may say about the cardinal:

The only all-red bird found in North America. Adult males are bright crimson all over with a prominent red crest. Females are also crested, but are dull rosy brown, lacking the males' bright red coloring. Common in woodland edges, along roadsides, and in backyards in the eastern two-thirds of North America. Frequents bird feeders where it eats sunflower seed. Both sexes emit a loud ringing chip! . . .

See how similar the two descriptions are? As you get more experience, you remember more things about the birds you know, and automatically look for more things on the birds you don't. Such observation skills are what identifying birds is all about. (See the section "Field marks: Front to back," later in this chapter, for more about using field marks to help identify birds.)

Look at the Bird, Not the Book

Sooner or later all bird watchers get a field guide. It's part of the trio of things that make up the activity called bird watching: **bird, binoculars, field guide,** oh, and **you,** I guess that's four things — a quartet!

Unless you're some kind of birding *savant,* born with encyclopedic bird knowledge, the steps you take to identify a bird go like this:

1. **See a bird.**

2. **Watch the bird for as long as you can, making notes on its appearance and behavior.**

    A good pair of binoculars helps immensely.

3. **Consult a field guide to confirm or find an identity for the bird.**

One of the pitfalls in using a field guide is the tendency of the beginning bird watcher to rely too heavily on the guide. Resist the temptation! Look at the bird for as long as you can. The picture of the bird in the book will always be there, but the actual living bird may only linger for a moment. Catch it while you can! The following sections help you remember what you see.

A mental checklist

Experienced bird watchers go through a mental checklist when looking at an unidentified bird: What is it doing? What size is it? What shape is it? What color? What are its main field marks? Does it have wingbars, an eyeline, a long tail?

You can do the same thing. Take a logical approach to looking at a bird. The first 10 or 20 times you have to make a conscious effort to remember all the things to look for, but after that, the checklist becomes automatic.

The following sections are designed to help make sure you see all the important bird features.

Talk to yourself

Ask yourself this question first: *What is most noticeable, most obvious about this bird?* Go ahead and talk to yourself. Memory is a leaky cup. When you're looking at the bird, you naturally believe you'll remember all the key points. It ain't so. By the time you get to the book, you may not remember whether the bird had wingbars or an eyering.

A useful trick is to say the bird's features (often called *field marks*) out loud while you mentally tick them off. This process works best if no one else is around, of course, although it can be helpful if you're sharing the moment with another observer who is as new to the game as you. By repeating the field marks out loud, you simplify later access to your memory bank, which, like all banks, is often closed when you need it most.

After you discover the *most* obvious clue to the bird's identity, look at the next most obvious clue, and then the next, and so on. As you gain experience, you mumble to yourself less and less. Experience makes much of the process so fast and automatic that vocal reminders aren't necessary. Until you reach that point, the social downside of being seen as a mutterer is offset by the advantage of being able to identify more birds.

Now your problem is how to remember all these clues.

Make notes, sketches, recordings . . .

Being a quick sketch artist is one way to help your brain remember the field marks of a mystery bird. This sketch requires no artistic skill whatsoever. Simply carry a small notepad and a pencil (with an eraser). Use these tools to jot down as much information as you can while the bird is still in front of you. Better yet, draw the outline of the bird, labeling the pertinent field marks as you go.

The high-tech version of this method is to carry a digital voice recorder with you. When you encounter an unfamiliar bird, you can whisper your observations into the microphone. Later, with a field guide in hand, you can play back the recording, listening to your notes (and reliving the moment).

First Impressions

First impressions are important. A small yellow bird is not a big gray bird and isn't even a small gray bird. The first impression is the outline that you use to organize the specifics. Sometimes the impression is enough by itself, but most often it serves to get you to the right three or four pages in the field guide (at which point you can start to nail down the bird's ID).

The first impression is made up of several fairly obvious steps. Look at the bird and record your impressions of the following features:

- ✔ The bird's most obvious characteristic (or two)
- ✔ The bird's behavior (what is the bird doing?)
- ✔ The bird's size, shape, color
- ✔ Whether landbird or waterbird

Pay attention to *where* you see the bird. The where is often a good clue to *what* the bird actually is. These things take a lot of time to explain (but less than a few seconds to do when you're actually looking at a bird).

The most obvious characteristic, simply stated, is what stands out about the bird. What made you notice it? The following sections cover bird characteristics that provide clues to a bird's identity.

Size — bigger than a breadbox?

Size matters. In birding lingo, *size* refers to the measurement of the bird from bill-tip to the end of the tail. Make a quick judgment, using whatever standard is familiar and comfortable.

> ✔ Is it bigger than a breadbox (or in this day and age, a cellular phone)?
>
> ✔ Is it about 6 inches, or is it more than a foot long?
>
> ✔ Is it shorter than your binoculars, or bigger than a small child?

Which method you use doesn't matter, as long as you have a reasonable idea of how big the bird is. Figure 4-3 compares relative sizes of birds.

You don't need to be precise. The difference between a 6-inch bird and a 5½-inch bird in the field is beyond most observers. Just get in the ballpark. Field guides aren't usually organized by size, but knowing how big or small the bird is helps to eliminate a lot of choices.

Figure 4-3: How big is big? From left to top right, comparing the sizes of a wild turkey, American crow, American robin, house finch, and ruby-throated hummingbird.

Pick a common bird — one you're very familiar with — as a size reference point: rock pigeon, starling, robin, and so forth. Then you can discern if a mystery bird is "smaller than a robin." Size is an excellent clue to identification.

Shape

By looking at a bird, even one silhouetted in poor light, you can make out its general shape. Shape is an important ID clue. You can use the same descriptive terms you use for humans: tall, lanky, thin, leggy, fat, squat, chunky, round, big-headed, small-headed, pointy-headed, and egotistical (oops, not that one!). You get the picture.

With a good idea of the bird's shape, you can narrow the possibilities, throwing out those species that the bird cannot possibly be.

Be aware that birds can and do change their shape. In cold weather, birds may puff out their feathers to increase heat retention. This puffing out process makes them appear larger than they actually are. Herons can fold their necks up until they appear to have no neck at all. A careful look at the bird helps you avoid being fooled.

Color

Color is one of the most easily grasped clues to a bird's identity. But color is not a foolproof, one-step ID tool. Why not? Because not all individual birds of a given species are the same color.

Variation exists among young (juvenile) and adult birds, among some males and females (called sexual dimorphism), and even among same-age, same-sex individuals. Further clouding the issue is the seasonal changing of plumage (feathers) that most birds go through.

An adult male American goldfinch in June looks like a brilliant golden and black jewel. The same bird in January wears colors of dull brownish yellow like a faded color photograph of the summer version.

Even with the confusing variables, you can use color to your advantage. When you see an unfamiliar bird, describe the color to yourself. Don't be afraid to mix the colors together. If the bird looks yellowish-greenish-brown to you, that's great! Better yet, try to remember what parts of the bird are a distinctive color. Does the bird have a dark cap? A rusty belly? White wing patches?

Remembering colors and where they appear on the bird is a great start to knowing more about field marks.

Wet or dry?

Birds are commonly separated into groups.

The easiest distinction is between *landbirds* and *waterbirds*. If the bird is swimming around in the middle of the lake, it probably isn't a sparrow. If the bird is sitting in a bush or hanging on your feeder, it probably isn't a duck.

Waterbirds include loons, grebes, seabirds, pelicans, cormorants, shorebirds (such as plovers and sandpipers), ducks, geese, swans, herons, egrets, ibises, cranes, rails, gulls, and terns, among others. Most of the waterbirds are located in the front of any field guide.

Landbirds include all the other birds you can think of.

In very few instances, this process of elimination won't work, but this method is always worth a try.

Field marks: Front to back

Start at the front end of the bird, the end with the bill, and work your way over the bird to the back end (the end without the bill). On many birds, the key field marks are found on the head. At the very least, the marks found on the head eliminate a lot of similar looking birds. Starting at the front/top end and working toward the tail is logical and helps you keep the information organized.

Pay (attention to) the bill

The bill is important. Birds are adapted to a specific way of life, and one of the most obvious adaptations is the bill. Bird bills come in a remarkable variety of shapes and sizes, each designed to a specific lifestyle. Is the bill long or short? Thick or thin? Hooked? Flattened? Broad? For example, sparrows have short, thick bills used for cracking seeds. Hawks have strong, hooked bills for tearing flesh. Herons have long, dagger-like bills for spearing fish. Figure 4-4 shows how different bills can be.

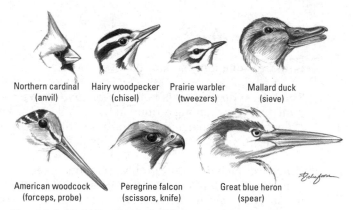

Northern cardinal (anvil)   Hairy woodpecker (chisel)   Prairie warbler (tweezers)   Mallard duck (sieve)

American woodcock (forceps, probe)   Peregrine falcon (scissors, knife)   Great blue heron (spear)

Figure 4-4: Bird bills with their different shapes resemble the tools named in parentheses. Use the tool names to help you identify the shape of a bill.

The bill usually tells you to which family or group your bird belongs. With a little practice, you can look at a bird's bill and say, automatically: "That's a chickadee." On some birds, such as pelicans and spoonbills, seeing the bill is virtually all you need. On others, the bill gets you to the right family of birds.

The head

More field marks appear on the heads of most birds than on any other part. Birds' heads can have eyerings, eyestripes, supercilia (don't worry, that's the plural of supercilium), and ear patches (on the side of the bird's head — birds' ears are usually concealed by feathers). In most cases, the field marks that matter on the head are stripes on the top (crown), eyerings, and a supercilium.

Look for obvious patterns, such as the crown stripes of a *white-crowned sparrow,* or the dark cap of a *black-capped chickadee.* Later, if the bird is still around, you can go back and look for subtleties.

Dozens of other field marks are associated with the head. Birds can be bald, bar-headed, beardless, bridled, browed, capped, cheeked, chinned, collared, crested, crowned, eared, eyed, faced, hooded, horned, masked, naped, necked (even red-necked!), nosed, plumed, polled, ringed, spectacled, striped, throated, tufted, and whiskered. And that's just the head.

Some body

Any reasonable person would conclude that a bird's body is one solid object. From the point of view of bird identification, however, a bird's body comes in two connected sections: the upperparts and the underparts. Many birds are named for their most noticeable body part, such as the *yellow-throated* warbler, or the *black-headed* grosbeak. Some birds are (stupidly) named for a marking that can only be seen on a bird held in the hand: *red-bellied* woodpecker and *ring-necked* duck are two examples. You never see either field mark unless you happen to be bird watching with the Hubble telescope.

Upperparts

The upperparts are the *back* and top surface of the *wings,* sometimes called the *mantle,* plus the area extending down to the base of the tail. The key field marks, if any exist on the upperparts, are usually found on the wings.

Many groups of birds (vireos and warblers, for instance) are divided into those that have wingbars and those that don't. Wingbars are pale stripes across the *shoulder* of the wing. On some birds, subtle distinctions exist in the size, width, and color of the wingbars, but you can be content simply to notice whether or not the wing has bars.

The back isn't vitally important to determining a bird's identity, but whether the back is streaked or plain is worth noting. If you can see the rump — the patch of feathers on the lower back, just above the tail — try to notice its color, too. You're in for a surprise the first time you see a yellow-rumped warbler!

Underparts

The underparts are the *breast, belly,* and *vent* (also called *undertail coverts*). In many birds, such as sparrows, noticing whether the breast is plain or streaked is important. In some hawks, the breast is *barred* (the streaks go sideways). Some birds have a breast that's one color and the belly another.

The underparts are unimportant for identification purposes on a number of birds, however. Ducks are a good example — ducks are usually seen swimming on a body of water and the underparts can only be described as, well, wet.

The tail

The tail can be a very helpful clue to a bird's identity. You most often note the tail on flying birds, but you can sometimes see the tail clearly when a bird is perched in a tree or hopping on the ground. For some species, a wagging or flicking movement of the tail is a diagnostic field mark. Tails can be relatively long or short, forked or square. On some birds, such as the *scissor-tailed* flycatcher, the tail is *the* field mark.

The legs

The legs are often overlooked, but sometimes are important for identification purposes. Bird feet aren't as helpful as ID tools, but they do tell you something about how the bird makes its living (see Figure 4-5). For example, hawks and owls have sharp, taloned feet used for grabbing and killing their prey. Ducks have short legs and webbed feet for swimming.

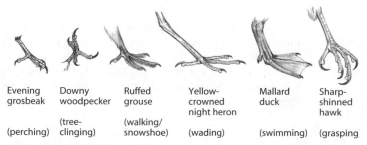

Evening grosbeak	Downy woodpecker	Ruffed grouse	Yellow-crowned night heron	Mallard duck	Sharp-shinned hawk
(perching)	(tree-clinging)	(walking/snowshoe)	(wading)	(swimming)	(grasping

Figure 4-5: Birds' feet can do specific tasks (see parentheses) and offer clues to a bird's identity.

Look for length and color of the legs. Herons have proportionately long legs for wading in deep water and long toes for support and balance; most land-birds have short legs. Color is often more important than length when looking at bird legs. Some birds, like lesser yellowlegs, are named for their leg color. The lesser yellowlegs is a medium-sized shorebird. This bird is one of a half dozen medium-sized shorebirds with yellow legs (including the confusingly similar greater yellowlegs), but then, the naming of birds isn't always logical.

Be careful with leg color. Birds that have been walking around in mud have black or brown legs. Birds that have been wading in oily water often appear to have red legs.

Plumage

Birds' feathers, called *plumage*, are what make birds different from all other animals on earth. And it's their feathers, or rather the color of their feathers, that make birds so compelling and so beautiful.

Because birds replace feathers as they wear out, you may see the same birds with slightly different plumage at different times during the year, just as you change from a suit and tie when you get home from the office, put on jeans and a sweatshirt to clean out the garage, and then don a tux to go to the ball.

Because worn-out feathers provide very little protection from cold and don't help much when a bird needs to fly, birds replace most of the feathers on their body every year. They do this by a process called *molt*. When birds molt, the old feathers fall out and a new set of unworn, unbroken feathers grows in. Most birds molt all of their feathers in the fall and a few feathers in the spring.

Sometimes, after molting, the bird's appearance changes. Greenish male scarlet tanagers change their drab feathers by growing in a set of brilliant red ones, offset by black wings. In late summer, many adult warblers begin a molt that makes them less boldly colored than they were just a few months prior. Bird molts provide another opportunity for bird watchers to study, or be frustrated by, birds.

Some birds, such as many male ducks, look different in the winter than they do in the summer. In some birds, such as many orioles, males look different than females. This isn't so that the males and females can tell each other apart. Birds never seem to have that problem. Rather, it reflects the different roles male and female birds have in the wild (sexism, I know, but the birds don't seem to mind).

In almost all birds, immature birds (young) look different from adults. Usually their plumage is duller and streakier. Although this difference typically lasts less than a year, in some cases (such as gulls and bald eagles), young birds can look different from adult birds for several years. The following plumage stages are typical of most birds:

- **Downy:** The fluffy usually white or gray feathers most baby birds have while they're still in the nest.

- **Juvenal:** The first real feathers a bird has after leaving the nest. Usually these feathers last about a month. Juvenile birds wear juvenal plumage.

- **Immature:** The feathers a bird wears for much of the first year of its life.

- **Adult:** The feathers the bird has after its first full year. This is the plumage commonly shown in field guides. Adult plumage often coincides with a bird's first breeding season. Reaching adult plumage can take as little as nine months, or in the case of bald and golden eagles and many gull species, several years.

Here are some seasonal plumages that adult birds have:

- **Breeding:** Breeding plumage is the equivalent of courting clothes. This plumage is often the bird's most colorful, especially in birds such as tanagers, many warblers, and ducks. Breeding plumage is commonly associated with adult males, whose bright feathers and loud song serve as an advertisement for a mate during the spring breeding season. Adult female birds, by and large, get the short end of the stick when it comes to flashy spring plumage. Female birds *do* get a new set of feathers each year, but not eye-catchingly brilliant ones.

> ✔ **Non-breeding:** Generically speaking, this is the bird's everyday dress — the plumage that birds are in when not in breeding season. It's also known as fall plumage, alternate plumage, and winter plumage.

These plumage terms are not something you need to memorize. They help you when you're using a field guide to identify a bird. Field guides show many different plumages for each bird species, so knowing some of the basic terminology is a bonus.

Behavior watching

Behavior (the bird's, not yours) can often lead you to the correct identification when all else fails. Chances are, the reason you're looking at a bird is because some aspect of its behavior attracted your attention. The bird flew past you, or you heard it sing, or saw it move high up on a branch. Because bird behavior is so easily observed, it's an excellent first-impression clue to a bird's identity.

The world of bird behavior encompasses a lot of interesting information. For identification purposes, here's a taste (an appetizer, if you will) of how behavior can be useful.

Bird behavior clues

Some birds constantly wag their tails (like palm warblers and phoebes); some (such as ruby-crowned kinglets) constantly flick their wings. Some birds hop, some walk, some creep, and some flutter. Some ducks dive while others feed by tipping over and sticking their backsides straight up in the air. Woodpeckers and nuthatches hop and scoot along tree trunks and branches searching for food. Hummingbirds hover over flowers to drink nectar. All are examples of bird behavior.

When gathering your first impression, ask yourself: What is this bird doing?

Bird sounds

Bird noises are an entirely separate area of endeavor. Birds have a wonderful and bewildering variety of sounds — from songs to calls to alarm notes. Some warblers have as many as eight or ten different types of vocalizations, depending on to whom they're talking and what mood they're in.

It's worth noting any distinctive noises the bird is making. Is the bird cawing like a crow? Croaking like a raven? Screaming like a jay? Mewing like a catbird?

Field Guide Time, at Last!

Okay, you've stared at the bird until you're glassy-eyed; you've catalogued (out loud) important field marks; you've watched the bird stretch, hop, and wiggle; and you've listened to the bird chip, warble, and sing. You've got enough evidence to solve this identification mystery. It's time to open the field guide and put a name on this thing.

When going to the field guide with a bird in mind that you hope to identify, you have two choices:

- If you have a general idea of the *kind* of bird you're looking for, you turn to the part of the guide that deals with that kind of bird.

- If you have *no clue* of what you're looking for, you have to flip through the whole guide page by page.

Option one — figuring out the kind of bird and looking for that type of bird in the guide — is the way to do it!

Option two is time consuming, and your memory slowly goes south on you with every page that passes. Before long, you have trouble distinguishing between what you actually saw in the field and what you're seeing in the book. Because waterbirds are in the first half of the field guide and landbirds are mostly in the second half, start by cutting the problem down.

Suppose that you've found the right section, and three or four pages of birds look pretty much alike. Glance quickly at each set of pictures to see if one of them jumps (or hops) off the page screaming, "It's me. It's me!" You've completed the journey, accomplishing the task at the heart of the bird-watching experience. You've put a name on the bird. Now you're ready to move on to the next challenge, and the next bird.

Not so fast!

A lot of people, including experts, make the mistake of stopping here. You need to take a few back-up steps:

1. **Keep looking!**

   A lot of people find a bird in the book that looks like the one in the bush and quit on the spot. They don't realize until much later that there's another bird, two pages later in the guide, that looks even *more* like the one they saw. Make sure you consider all the possibilities.

2. **Don't cram the bird into the picture!**

   Well, the bird you saw looks a lot like the one on page 235 of the field guide, except you didn't see the big white patch on the wings. Oh well, you may think, you probably just overlooked it. Sorry, that won't hold up in court. It's likely that you're looking at the wrong bird in the field guide.

   If you find yourself working too hard to explain field marks that don't quite fit, you probably have made a mistake.

3. **Look at the map!**

   You may not know which birds are supposed to be in your backyard and which ones are only found on the other side of the continent (or which ones only visit your area during a certain season of the year). That's why field guides have range maps. Isn't that brilliant? What's not clear is why so many people never look at them. Maybe it's the same unexplained phenomenon as why men never want to stop the car to ask directions.

Home on the range

Range can solve a lot of identification problems. If you have a chickadee coming to your feeder, and you live in California, you can take one glance at the map and eliminate Carolina chickadee. If you confidently have identified the small brown bird in your Virginia backyard as a wrentit (a western bird), you may have made a mistake. So, after you think you know what you're looking at, check the map and make sure the bird can be seen in your area. If the bird doesn't occur in your area, go back to the pictures and try again.

Birds have wings and tend to use them. They are very mobile creatures.

Just because your field guide's map says the bird you've iden- tified shouldn't occur where you're seeing it, that doesn't mean that it can't happen. Either you've misidentified the bird or the bird misread the map in the field guide. A bird far from its normal range is called a *vagrant* or an *accidental*. If you think your bird is one of these, ask another bird watcher to help you confirm the identification. Finding a vagrant bird is an exciting experience.

Don't ever be afraid to ask questions of other bird watchers, particularly if they're more experienced than you. Ask for help with a tricky bird ID, or ask "How did you know that was a . . . ?" You pick up lots of great ID tips this way. And you'll probably make a few friends, too.

If All Else Fails . . .

If all else fails, start over. You may find it frustrating, but go back and look at the bird again, assuming it's still around. If it isn't, go on to the next bird. You don't have to identify every bird you see. No one does, and no one is keeping score. This process is supposed to be fun! Smile! Do what every other bird watcher does — grade yourself on a very generous curve.

Mistakes happen. . . . Big deal!

Three outcomes are possible when you attempt to identify a bird:

✔ **You get it right — you correctly identify the bird.**

It may take a while before you're absolutely sure, but you *will* get it right.

> ✔ **You don't figure it out, and the bird takes off before you can solve the mystery.**
>
> You don't forget the one that gets away. When you see it again, you'll be ready.
>
> ✔ **You get it wrong — you (gasp!) misidentify the bird.**
>
> You may not realize it at first, but as you see more birds and become more confident in your identification, you know that you got it wrong.

The newer you are to bird watching, the more likely the result will be #2 or #3. Because we all hate to admit failure, #3 will be more common than #2, whether you know it or not. You will — and this is an absolute certainty — misidentify birds when you first start out. In fact, you'll do it for the rest of your bird-watching life. I misidentified a rock pigeon yesterday as a Cooper's hawk. My wife rubbed it in, but she didn't leave me. (She did point at me and whisper something in our daughter's ear, however.)

Don't worry about it if you misidentify a bird. The Fate of the Free World doesn't hang in the balance. Misidentifying birds isn't a social crime equivalent to dipping into the collection plate or secretly dumping your leaves into your neighbor's yard. Misidentifying birds is part of the process of becoming a bird watcher. Eventually, you'll correctly identify almost all the birds that you see.

Chapter 5

Watching Bird Behavior

*A*nything that a bird does can be considered part of its behavior, and when you think about it, birds do a lot. They fly, sing, forage for food, perform mating displays, select mates, breed, fight, build nests, lay eggs, preen, bathe, and do lots of other stuff.

Bird behavior provides you, the bird watcher, with two primary things: entertainment and information. The entertainment is easy to understand: It's neat to watch birds do their thing. The information aspect of bird behavior provides clues to a bird's identity and gives us insight into the lives of birds. Of course, birds get lots more out of their behavior than we, the watchers, do.

What Is Bird Behavior?

Bird behavior, at its most basic, is simply a bird being a bird. Anything and everything a bird does is bird behavior. Even a bird, say a song sparrow, sitting still for a moment on a sun-drenched perch on a chilly spring morning — apparently doing nothing — provides an example of bird behavior. The bird is sunbathing, catching some solar warmth, just as we humans do on a sunny day.

Birds behave more like humans than you may think. They form reasonably loyal pairs between males and females (though studies show there is some avian hanky-panky), raise mostly helpless young (babies that cannot immediately feed and fend for themselves), defend their home territories, have food preferences, and so on. Some *ornithologists* (scientists who study birds professionally) speculate that it's because birds form loyal pair bonds that we humans are so fascinated with their lives. If you've ever watched a pair of birds nest in your backyard, you'll know what I mean. You get pretty attached to those birds. They become *your* birds!

Some common (and easily observed) examples of bird behavior include foraging, bathing and preening, singing, territoriality, courtship, nest building, roosting, flocking, and migration.

Bird behavior is easy to see, if you're aware of the opportunities you have to see it. When you see a bird's activity that attracts you, try to figure out what the behavior is. A bird's behavior is what allows it to survive life in a harsh environment. Don't you wonder how birds survive in extreme weather? How would *you* like to spend all day in the freezing rain and then have to keep warm all night when the moisture freezes into ice? Under such conditions, birds change their behavior to improve their chances of survival:

- ✔ They move around less to save energy.
- ✔ They may spend more time at a reliable food source, whether natural or artificial (such as a bird feeder).
- ✔ They puff up their feathers to trap and retain body heat.
- ✔ They seek shelter.

These changes in behavior are not decisions they make; these behavior changes are instinctual. They're a response to the stimulus of the weather.

Foraging

Foraging is the act of finding food. All birds have a distinct means of getting food. Robins scamper along on the lawn looking for earthworms (I have yet to see a robin standing in line at the bait shop), swallows swoop through the air catching flying insects, and woodpeckers hitch up tree trunks and branches looking for insects to excavate from the bark.

Birds can be generalists in their foraging, looking anywhere and everywhere for food. Good examples of generalists are European starlings and ring-billed gulls, both of which can be found seeking food in a variety of places, from shoreline to city park to fast-food–restaurant dumpster.

Birds can also be very specific in their foraging techniques. Members of the sapsucker family have an interesting foraging method. These birds drill a series of holes in tree trunks or branches. These holes cause the tree to produce protective sap, which oozes out of the holes in small amounts. It's the same concept that humans use to tap maple trees to make maple syrup. Later, the sapsuckers return to consume the sap. Other birds have learned about sapsucker holes, too. Many warblers, hummingbirds, and other small songbirds visit the holes for sap and to dine upon the insects that the sweet, sticky sap attracts.

Singing and Sound-Making

Bird song plays an important role in courtship and territoriality among birds. Although the males do the singing in most, but not all, bird species (to attract a female for mating), all birds make other sounds, too, such as chip notes, alarm notes, scolding notes, and even non-vocal sounds such as wing whistling (a sound made by air passing through a flying bird's wing feathers). If you've ever heard a mourning dove launch suddenly into flight (as when scared), you've probably heard the whistling sound the dove's wings make.

Some wren species keep the sexes equal when it comes to vocalizations by performing duet singing. These songs, performed in tandem from separate locations, are thought to help maintain the pair's bond with each other. Wrens also have many contact calls — short whistles or peeps that serve to say: "I'm fine, dear, and I'm over here eating spider eggs in the wood pile." Sort of like calling home just to check in.

Vocal mimicry among birds is a fascinating thing. One of North America's best mimics is the northern mockingbird, which has been recorded imitating the songs and calls of more than 30 other bird species within a ten-minute span. If you have mockingbirds near you, you may have been lucky enough to hear the male sing his full repertoire all night long during a full moon. They borrow bits and snippets of other birds' songs and blab day and night.

Another neat example of birds using vocalizations is the blue jay's crafty method of clearing off the bird feeder. I didn't believe this until I saw it myself at our feeders. A jay (or several jays) sees a feeding station crowded with birds. Instead of flying in and muscling its way to the seed (which could result in an injury), one of the jays gives an alarm call. Some jays even imitate the scream of a hawk. The effect this has on the smaller feeder visitors is akin to that of a person yelling "Fire!" in a packed movie theater. The little birds scram, and the jays take over the feeder. How's that for bird brains?

Bathing/Preening

If you were to go without a bath for a few — make that a *phew* — days or a few weeks, your family and friends would start making comments about it, such as "Plumbing not working at your house?" If a bird were to avoid bathing for the same amount of time, it might not survive. The personal hygiene of birds is a matter of life and death. Feathers that aren't clean don't function efficiently, either in flight or in protecting the body from weather and wear and tear. And let's not forget looks. Gaudy-plumaged males need to look good if they hope to attract a mate.

Several kinds of bathing behavior exist among birds, but the most common are water bathing, dust bathing, and sunbathing.

Water bathing

Water bathing is the most common behavior, and it can be easily observed if you offer water to birds in your yard.

Birds don't bathe like humans do. Most birds that bathe in water prefer to wade into water that's a few inches deep and then splash the water onto their bodies. After bathing for a few minutes and getting thoroughly soaked, a bird flies to a safe perch to preen.

Preening is just like a bird combing its hair, but instead of using a comb or brush, birds use their bills. Preening smoothes down the feathers and feather edges and removes dirt and parasites from the feathers. Preening also allows the bird to distribute natural oil over its feathers. This oil, which comes from the bird's oil gland located at the base of the tail, helps give feathers durability and a certain amount of water resistance.

Birds don't rely exclusively on our bird baths for bathing. They use any shallow or splashing source of water, including puddles, ponds, sprinklers, and even the water caught in leaves after a rainstorm. In fact, many bird species use a rainstorm as an opportunity to take a shower.

Dust bathing

Certain species of birds, such as quail, pheasants, grouse, and turkeys, prefer to dust bathe, using fine dust or loose dirt to help keep their feathers clean.

"But how can they get clean in the dirt?" I hear you ask. Ornithological studies have shown that dust bathing improves feather fluffiness and also discourages or dislodges parasites, along with reducing excess moisture and oil.

Sunbathing

Birds also enjoy bathing in bright, hot sunlight (just as humans do). If you watch some of your familiar backyard birds during warm, sunny weather, particularly following a cloudy, rainy, or cool spell, you may see this behavior.

A sunbathing bird doesn't get out the shades and suntan lotion. Instead, it spreads out its wings and tail and raises its feathers so that the sunlight strikes its bare skin in several places. Sunbathing birds often sprawl on the ground or on rooftops, looking dazed, their bills agape. Many theories exist to explain what birds get from this; these theories include increased vitamin production from the sunlight, increased warmth, and a benefit in driving parasites from the bird's back to its breast, where these pests can be preened away.

Anting

One fascinating feather-cleaning method employed by some birds is called anting. There are two types of anting: active anting and passive anting. In active anting, birds crush ants with their bills and wipe the crushed ants through their feathers. Ornithologists believe that the acidic juices of the crushed ants help the birds ward off feather mites, lice, and other parasites. In passive anting, a bird lies down on the ground on or near an anthill, with wings and feathers spread apart, and lets the ants crawl all over it. It's believed that the ants seek out and remove parasites from the bird's plumage. Worldwide, more than 200 bird species have been recorded as engaging in anting behavior. Among the North American species that use anting are American robin, American crow, blue jay, northern cardinal, evening grosbeak, and purple finch.

Dating and Mating: Courtship

Remember your first date? Remember that head-over-heels, dizzy feeling you got? You planned out the whole thing, right down to the wedding attendants. Okay. You can stop now. Let's talk about birds. Sorry to distract you. . . .

Bird courtship is a spring phenomenon across most of North America, except for the southernmost reaches where the climate is warm year-round. Most of what birds do in the spring involves courtship, either directly or indirectly, including setting up territories, singing, performing visual displays, and taking off in hot pursuit.

Male ruby-throated hummingbirds perform an interesting courtship display flight. When they locate a female hummer perched nearby, the males zoom above her in a swooping, U-shaped arc. This is called the *pendulum display* because the pattern resembles the path of a ticking clock's pendulum. During the display, the male chatters, his beating wings buzz, and he tries to maneuver himself so the tiny feathers on his *gorget* (throat) catch the sunlight and show off his ruby-colored throat to the watching female.

Have you ever noticed how, on warm days during the late winter and early spring, the birds seem to get much more active? This activity is caused by the birds' raised hormonal levels, which are affected by warmer temperatures and increased sunlight. It's a kind of avian spring fever.

Signs of spring on our farm are first apparent in early February when the red-shouldered hawks begin forming pairs. Soon after, our bluebirds begin peeking into their nest boxes, singing and waving their wings in courtship display.

The first thing a migrant bird does upon returning to its nesting grounds is select a territory and begin singing. Singing serves to attract a mate and to repel potential challengers for both mate and territory.

Bird courtship displays are designed to show off the male's color and markings to his best advantage: the male American redstart fans its wings and tail to show off the bright orange patches that would otherwise be concealed. Male meadowlarks puff out their bright yellow breast feathers and sing from an exposed perch. Even male rock pigeons put on a show, bowing and cooing while fanning their tails and inflating their necks to show off iridescent feathers.

At your backyard feeder, you may observe another type of courtship behavior, especially if you have cardinals. The male cardinal selects a seed (it has to be just right, I'm sure) and feeds it to his mate in what is sometimes called a *courtship kiss*. When receiving the seed, the female cardinal quivers her wings in excitement, just like a fledgling bird begging for food. The male cardinal continues to feed his mate while she incubates eggs on the nest, as do many songbirds.

Nest Building

Birds can be classified by their nest types as follows:

- ✔ **Ground nesters** make their nests on the ground; some create a nest, some use just a shallow scrape, and some don't improve the nest site at all. Examples of ground-nesting birds are turkeys, some ducks, larks, towhees, and most shorebirds.

✔ **Cup nesters** create the stereotypical bird's nest woven out of plant materials. Most North American bird species construct open-cup nests. Examples of cup nesters are robins, most warblers, tanagers, most flycatchers, most hawks, and hummingbirds.

✔ **Cavity nesters** use hollow, enclosed areas, such as a hollow tree, for nesting. Woodpeckers create their own cavities by excavating holes in trees. The excavation of a nest hole is an important part of woodpecker courtship, so woodpeckers create new cavities each spring for nesting. Old woodpecker nests are used in subsequent years by many other cavity nesting species, such as titmice, chickadees, bluebirds, great crested flycatchers, some ducks, and owls.

With a few exceptions, almost all birds build structures for nesting, often using specific materials. Robins use mud in their nests, chickadees use moss, tree swallows use white feathers, gnatcatchers and hummingbirds use lichens and spider webs, while chipping sparrows line their nests with hair.

Nest-building behavior can include many activities. Gathering of materials, such as grass or sticks, site selection by mated pairs, and the actual building of the nest are all readily observable examples of this behavior. Find a bird that you know nests in your part of the continent and watch its activity during the spring months (see Figure 5-1). See if you can pick up clues that tell you if it's nesting in your immediate area.

The wooded hillsides on our farm are home to several pairs of ovenbirds, a ground-nesting warbler that's named for the way its nest is constructed. Ovenbird nests resemble tiny Dutch ovens — a domed cup with a small entrance on one side. Ovenbirds build these nests on the ground, often near a woodland path or road. The materials include moss, twigs, dead grasses, rootlets, and animal hair. A roof of dead leaves helps both to conceal the nest on the forest floor, and to keep out the rain.

You can watch birds in your yard collect nesting material by offering them short pieces (3 inches or shorter) of soft string, yarn, and human or pet hair. Scatter it about your yard in obvious places, or offer it in an unused, wire-basket suet feeder and watch the birds investigate. When my beloved wife goes to the beauty salon (and I'm at the beauty saloon) for her annual big haircut, she asks for the clippings of her own hair. I know this seems weird, but that's my wife (hey, she married *me!*). She brings the hair home in a plastic bag and scatters it around the lawn and garden. In the fall, we find several different chipping sparrow nests lined with her hair. She gets a kick out of that.

Figure 5-1: An ovenbird at its Dutch oven–shaped nest.

Female birds are the nest builders in most species with little or no help from the male. In some species, such as chickadees, titmice, hawks, and eagles, the males help out with the building. House wrens and marsh wrens are different in that the males construct several different nests from which the females select their favorite for actual use.

Some ground-nesting birds, such as nighthawks, killdeer, and terns, build no nests at all; rather, they rely on the natural camouflage of their speckled eggs to protect the nest, which may be no more than a shallow scrape in rocky or sandy soil.

Defending My Space: Territoriality

Much of the same behavior that birds use in courtship is also associated with territoriality. Only this behavior is redirected at interlopers, rivals, and even potential predators rather than at potential mates.

A bird's *territory* is that physical area that a bird defends against other members of its own species. Bird territories can be defended year-round by nonmigratory birds, such as mockingbirds, or as temporarily as the small spot of ground that a sanderling defends while feeding along the ocean beach. Territories can range from vast amounts of land to small zones a few feet square.

During the spring and summer breeding season, you notice most territorial behavior among birds. This is when males compete for mates, for prime territories, and for dominance over rivals with nearby territories.

Examples of territorial behavior include the males' singing from prominent song perches, such as the top of a tree; fighting among rivals along territorial boundaries; chasing interlopers from a territory; and scolding, which is a harsher, less musical vocalization than singing.

Tips for Watching Bird Behavior

If the definition of bird behavior is anything that a bird does, then behavior watching is defined as *watching* anything that a bird does. It doesn't get much simpler than that.

Behavior watching gains popularity with bird watchers as they become more familiar with certain common bird species. Backyard watchers especially enjoy observing the behavior of those species that regularly appear in their yards and at their feeders.

You can easily give behavior watching a try with the next bird you see. Focus your attention on observing what the bird does, and see if you can guess why it's doing what it's doing.

Birds aren't little people. Although it's both fun and tempting to *anthropomorphize* — attribute human traits, such as feelings of love, joy, hate, and so on, to birds and other non-human creatures — it's not realistic or accurate. Bird behavior is almost always a reaction to a stimulus. A bird is hungry, so it looks for food. When it finds food, it doesn't stop to think, "Boy, am I feeling full. I ate too much. I need to watch my weight!" Birds just act and react, despite how much we'd like to think they're really rational and feeling, like us humans. By the way, you should do as I say, not as I do.

When and where to look

Birds are most active during the early morning hours and in the late afternoon, so naturally these are the times when behavior is most evident. But behavior can happen anytime and anywhere. Nearly all owls are most active at night. Their daytime behavior consists of sleeping. In the summer months, male songbirds sing most of the day, making this behavior pretty easy to observe and to hear.

I suggest that you start by looking for bird behavior among your backyard birds. Or look at a nearby park, where ducks may be on a pond or herons stalking fish along the edges. Even rock pigeons (rock doves) in the city have amazing and easy-to-observe behaviors, such as courtship, fancy mate-impressing display flights, territorial fights, and a variety of vocalizations. Bird behavior, like birds, is everywhere.

What to look for

Because almost anything that a bird does can be classified as behavior, choose an easy-to-observe bird and watch it for signs of interesting behavior. For example:

- Birds at rest may engage in preening, or they may hunker down and tuck their heads into the scapular or shoulder feathers.

- Foraging birds use many methods to get food, including gleaning from tree trunks and branches, flycatching, probing in the ground, excavating in wood, diving into water, hovering, scraping, prying, and even scaring prey into the open by flashing their tail and wing feathers.

✔ Birds in flight can exhibit behaviors such as predator evasion, elaborate courtship displays, migration, and territoriality.

When you see birds in action, ask yourself what it means. Why is the bird doing that? Lots of bird behavior is repetitive, so you may have more than one chance to catch a certain behavior and figure it out for yourself.

My favorite time of the year for watching bird behavior is the springtime. This is when the migrants return from the tropics, and all the birds, even our resident species, get sort of crazy with the onset of the breeding season. The morning is full of bird song, and the trees and fields around our farm are alive with all kinds of foraging, preening, singing, and chasing behavior. I love to pick out one bird and try to watch it for as long as possible. I get to see into this one individual bird's world — watch it live its life — while the bird is totally oblivious to me and my world. Time spent in this way is incredibly interesting, and wonderfully peaceful.

I wish I could be out birding right now. But it's February and snowing. And I'm sitting in front of the computer, writing this book. Do me a favor. Go out and see a few birds for me, will you?

Keeping notes

An interesting part of behavior watching is keeping notes on what you observe. For many years, we've featured a column in *Bird Watcher's Digest* on bird behavior, and it's always among the most avidly read parts of our magazine. Of special interest is the feature at the end of the column in which reader questions and observations are shared and, when possible, explanations of bird behavior are given. Over the years, we've gotten some incredible observations, mostly from careful observers who took notes on what they were seeing.

Keeping notes is very simple. Carry a small notebook with you when you plan to watch birds. When something unusual occurs, you're ready to record your observations while they're still fresh in your mind. Here are some things to consider when recording your observations:

- ✔ What species is the bird?
- ✔ What sex is the bird or birds?
- ✔ What season of the year is it?
- ✔ What is the time of day or night?
- ✔ How would you describe the bird's behavior?
- ✔ What do you think was the cause or purpose of the behavior (mating, courtship, foraging, and so on)?
- ✔ Describe the habitat or location in which the behavior was occurring (berry-filled tree, deep woods, at the bird feeders, and so on).
- ✔ Make notes about any other factors that may have affected the behavior (weather, contested food source, presence of predators, and so on).

If you enjoy keeping notes on behavior, you'll really enjoy referring to these notes in the future, long after the actual incident has faded from memory. Your behavior notes provide a wealth of information.

Behavior as an ID Tool

The behavior of birds is very useful in determining a bird's identity. Many bird species have distinctive behavior, such as tail wagging or flicking; certain styles or patterns of flight; feeding styles, such as probing in the mud or flycatching in midair; and, of course, all types of vocalizations that can be used as tools for bird identification.

Suppose that you see a bird that you can't identify right away — perhaps it's a life bird for you (one you've never seen before in your life). You can tell it's a small yellowish warbler. It's spring, so you know that warblers are present as they migrate through your area. This warblerlike bird is flitting from low branches to the grassy ground. All the while it's pumping its tail up and down as it forages. You catch a glimpse of a rusty patch on the bird's head just before the bird flies away. You make a mental note about the bird, particularly about the wagging tail. Later on, when you look at your field guide, you find several yellowish warblers that can be found in your area in spring, but only one with a rusty cap and a constantly moving tail: a palm warbler. Bird behavior was the clinching clue in that bird's identification.

When you see a strange bird, one that's not immediately recognizable to you, look for signs of unusual behavior, along with the bird's physical field marks. Behavior is a great ID tool, and one many bird watchers forget to use.

Bird behavior keeps veteran bird watchers interested long after they've exhausted the possibilities for seeing new birds every time out. If you're interested in finding out more about bird behavior, I have two suggestions:

✔ Watch as many birds as you can at every opportunity. Careful watchers see lots of amazing behavior.

✔ Consult additional publications, which can be excellent sources for insight into the behavior of birds.

I have to stop writing now. The red-bellied woodpecker is hammering on the side of my house, near the kitchen window. He knows that when he does this, I'll come outside to refill the peanut feeder and the suet feeder. It's his way of getting me to respond to his behavior. I think he has me pretty well trained. Don't you?

Chapter 6

Bird Sounds: News and Entertainment

• •

• •

*B*irds are very noisy creatures when they want to be. This fact is both good and bad news for you, the bird watcher. The news is good because when a bird is making noise, you can more easily locate it and perhaps identify the bird without needing to see it.

The bad part about bird sounds is that — to the beginner — the vast array of songs and calls made by birds on a spring morning can be unbelievably daunting. Experiencing bird sounds can seem like you may never figure out who's singing what. But take heart, I share some tricks of the trade to help you sort things out.

A bird uses two primary senses, sight and sound, to communicate with other birds. *Sight communication* involves colorful plumage and plumage patterns, as well as physical movement such as flight displays. *Sound communication* includes the vast array of sounds that birds can make. Most (but not all) of these sounds are vocalizations, which are generically called *bird song*.

In this chapter I discuss the basic types of bird sounds and how birds use these to communicate. And I tell you how to begin understanding bird songs and calls, especially as they pertain to bird identification.

Types of Bird Sounds

Birds make these basic kinds of sounds: songs, calls, and non-vocal sounds. All three types of sounds have a purpose, but not all birds make all three sounds. Most bird species, however, rely on songs and calls. Some species — such as woodpeckers and some game birds, such as the ruffed grouse — lack the vocal skills of, say, the warblers, and rely on other means to make noise and attract attention. And bird sounds are all about getting noticed.

Bird songs

Strictly defined, *bird song* is a repetitive pattern of musical notes or vocalizations. Birds produce their songs using a complex muscular organ called the syrinx, which is roughly analogous to our larynx. The syrinx allows birds to produce beautiful vocal sounds. The syrinx also allows birds to produce several tones at one time, unlike most humans who can only produce a single tone at a time. When recorded and played back at a slow rate, the simple *chickadee-dee-dee* call of the black-capped chickadee is found to be composed of several harmonic tones, all sung at once.

Among North American birds, true song (that is, a complex vocalization designed to attract a mate) is almost exclusively performed by adult male birds in, or en route to, their established territories during the spring and summer months, which is the breeding or nesting season. The bird species that perform elaborate vocalizations are known as songbirds, but this label can be a little misleading. A northern bobwhite is not considered a songbird, but I love listening to this bird's cheery whistle.

Spring song starts earlier in the southern parts of the continent than it does in the northern parts. Spring song in southern Florida may begin in earnest in late January, while folks in the Rocky Mountain regions of Colorado, or those in New Hampshire, may wait until early April for the birds to get going vocally. In other parts of the West, where the seasonal differences in temperature and weather are not as great, the advent of spring song is strung out over many months.

Bird song reaches its crescendo across much of the continent during spring migration when birds that are already in territories (early-arriving migrants and resident or nonmigratory species) are joined by passing migrants. These migrants — thrushes, vireos, warblers, orioles, and tanagers — are singing their way northward to establish territories of their own.

Watch the birds in your backyard in early spring. As they sort out their turf boundaries, the males begin to perform most of their singing from favorite spots within their territories. These prominent locations are called *song perches.* Males use song perches to display themselves to the best advantage, both to potential mates and to nearby rivals. You can find the song perches in your backyard at the tops of trees, at the peak of a roof, or perhaps from the top of a brushpile. Song perches offer a reliable place to look for territorial male birds during the breeding season.

Bird calls

Not every vocal sound that a bird makes is a song. Many short chips, whistles, trills, twitters, and chirps are uttered by birds. All of these sounds, referred to as *bird calls,* have a communication role among birds.

Calls are used by birds in a variety of ways. Among the uses of calls are

- To keep contact among the members of a flock, family, or pair of birds
- To warn off predators
- To signal food

The primary difference between bird songs and bird calls is that calls are much shorter in duration and may be less musical. Some birds, such as the American crow, don't have very musical songs, but they do possess an array of calls. I think of bird calls as being strictly functional, like a tool, whereas true bird song sounds more artistic, more musical.

All birds, including very young birds (nestlings), use call notes for communication. If you listen to the bird sounds in your yard, you can pick out the sounds that are obvious call notes, and those that are actual, full-fledged song.

Some of the calls you may encounter among the common birds in your area are the *pit-pit-pit!* alarm call of the American robin; the *pick!* call of the downy woodpecker; and the *chicka-dee-dee-dee* call of the black-capped chickadee, or of the very similar Carolina chickadee, found in the southeastern portions of the United States.

Non-vocal sounds

Can you sing? Not everybody can. And if you've been to Karaoke Night lately, you've had a painful reminder of this fact. Not all birds can sing, either. Some birds have evolved, over the eons, to make their courtship and territorial points using non-vocal sounds. These sounds may be produced by specialized feather shafts that whistle in flight (woodcocks and some duck species have these feather shafts), or by specialized displays that involve a booming sound produced by flapping wings (the male ruffed grouse's drumming), or by some other specialized behavior, such as a woodpecker's drumming on hollow trees to make noise.

Mimics

Birds are the only living creatures, other than humans, capable of imitating sounds that they weren't born to produce. This ability to learn and imitate strange sounds is called *vocal mimicry,* and the birds that can do it are called *mimics.*

The almost-indisputable champion of vocal mimicry among North American birds is the northern mockingbird. How good are mockingbirds at singing and mimicry? One mocker was heard to perform the songs of more than 50 different species in one hour. Most mockingbirds have a repertoire that includes two dozen or more songs and calls. Some have learned to imitate doorbells, ringing telephones, whistles, and even the notes of a piano.

Other excellent mimics in our midst include the gray catbird, brown thrasher (some bird people believe the thrasher, which can have as many as 1,000 song bits in its repertoire, is the king of the mimics), blue jay, yellow-breasted chat, and the European starling. The mockingbird, thrashers, and catbird are all members of the genus *Mimidae,* which is Latin for *mimic.*

Song as an Identifier

Bird song is a very useful identification tool for bird watchers. I can't count the number of times that bird song has been the clinching clue to a bird's identity, especially when I've had a less-than-perfect look at the bird. I remember the song or call, and later consult a field guide for a description of the song, or better yet, listen to an actual recording of the bird's song.

In fact, some birds are most readily identified by their vocalizations. One example is the group of drab gray-green birds known as the *Empidonax* flycatchers. *Empidonax* is Latin (the literal translation is "mosquito king") for the group of small, indistinctly marked flycatchers. The Acadian, willow, alder, least, and yellow-bellied flycatchers live in the eastern portions of North America. Western bird watchers get to thrill to the calls of the least and willow flycatchers, as well as the Hammond's, dusky, Pacific slope, cordilleran, buff-breasted, and gray flycatchers.

These flycatchers are so similar in appearance that most bird watchers rely on the calls of each for positive identification. When faced with a non-vocal "Empid," as these birds are generically known, birders everywhere do one of three things: make an educated guess, shrug and list the bird only as Empid species, or sit and wait patiently for the bird to make a peep.

Each bird you encounter is an individual, so don't be surprised if you encounter differences in the songs you hear from two members of the same species — just as each person has a distinctive voice and even an accent. Bird watchers listening to recordings of bird songs often remark, "That doesn't sound like our (wren/warbler/whatever) at all!" That's because birds from different parts of the continent have different dialects, sometimes even different songs. Listen for common characteristics that give you a composite aural picture of the species' song: pitch, tone, pattern. Is the song ringing? Sibilant? Syncopated? Thin and wiry or rich and chortling?

You'll have lots of situations in which you, my fellow bird watcher, will hear but not see birds. At night, owls and nightjars (whippoorwills, nighthawks, and their kin) will be calling, but offer you little to look at. There will be thick vegetation, fog, poor light. There will be treetop-singing warblers. There will be annoyingly persistent singers that you *just can't seem to locate!* The picture I'm painting here is that you will greatly benefit from opening your ears to the wonders (and usefulness!) of bird songs. All you have to do is listen!

Start with a Reference Bird

To begin deciphering and recognizing bird songs, I suggest you pick a *reference bird.* Choose a common species, preferably one that sings regularly in your area. Perhaps this bird is a cardinal if you live in the East, or a white-crowned sparrow if you live in the West. The American robin is reasonably common all across the continent, so maybe the robin works as a reference bird for you.

Listen to your reference bird's call and songs as often as you can. Soon, you become familiar with this species' vocalizations, and you're able to pick them out if they're singing, no matter where you are. This practice establishes a good reference point for your future bird-song adventures.

When you next hear a bird song that you can't identify, use the song of your reference bird as a comparison. If your reference bird is a robin, which has a rich, throaty, warbling song, compare the mystery bird's song to that of the robin. Is it thinner-sounding? Is it harsher? More musical? While you're making the comparison, try to make visual contact with the mystery bird.

 If you're just beginning with bird songs, I suggest you start by trying to sort out the early spring songs of common birds in and around your backyard. Get outside and listen before all the spring migrants come through, and before all the summer nesters begin to set up territories. Believe me, you have fewer songs to sort out in the early spring than at the height of migration in your area. The peak period of bird migration varies greatly from north to south and east to west. For much of North America, spring migration starts early in the year — as early as late January — and ends in mid-to-late June. Knowing the songs of your locally common and resident (nonmigratory) birds gives you a great head start later when these songs are mixed with dozens of others. Knowing these few songs, you can put them aside and concentrate on the new ones you're hearing.

A phrase to remember

Pleased to meetcha, Miss Beecher! is one of my all-time favorite phrases used to describe a bird song — in this case, a chestnut-sided warbler. The genius of this phrase is that it not only *sounds* like what the bird sings, it's weird enough that you're not going to forget it immediately.

Field guides to the birds invariably include a description of the vocalizations of each species. These descriptions may be straightforward ("a buzzy trill ending on an upward phrase") or poetic ("a melodic series of ethereal, flutelike notes"). But my favorites are the old-fashioned "sounds like the bird is saying" descriptions, such as *Quick! Three beers!* (olive-sided flycatcher), *Drink your tea!* (eastern towhee — formerly called the rufous-sided towhee), and *Spring of the year!* (eastern meadowlark).

Table 6-1 lists some phrases that may help you remember a bird by its song.

Table 6-1	Bird Songs to Remember
Name of Bird	Sounds Like
Red-eyed vireo	Here I am. Look at me. I'm up here!
Yellow-throated vireo	Helen, Helen! Come here!
White-throated sparrow	Old Sam Peabody, Peabody, Peabody! (or) Oh Sweet Canada, Canada, Canada!
Carolina wren	Teakettle, teakettle, teakettle!
Barred owl	Who cooks for you? Who cooks for you-all?
California quail	Chi-ca-go!
Olive-sided flycatcher	Quick! Three beers!
Black-throated blue warbler	I am so lay-zee!
Yellow warbler	Sweet, sweet, I'm so sweet!
Indigo bunting	Fire! Fire! Where? Where? There! There! Put it out! Put it out!
Eastern (rufous-sided) towhee	Drink your tea!
Golden-crowned sparrow	Oh dear me!
Eastern meadowlark	Spring of the year!

As you become more familiar with the songs of the birds you hear, feel free to come up with your own descriptions. How goofy they are doesn't matter, as long as they help you to remember.

Is there a pattern here?

Another method for remembering a bird's song is to tie the rhythm or cadence of the song to a pattern. A good example of this is the description used for the song of the American goldfinch, one often sung in flight: *Po-ta-to chip! Po-ta-to chip!* For my money, what the goldfinch is singing does *not* sound like the actual phrase "potato chip" but the rhythmic pattern of that phrase and the bird's song are unmistakably similar. "Potato chip" is an excellent reminder of the song's pattern. And because potato chips are a bird watcher's staple when out in the field, the phrase is never far from your mind.

Birding by Ear

With experience you'll become more comfortable with your ability to identify birds by their songs, calls, and sounds. Getting experience is the same as getting directions on how to get to Carnegie Hall: *practice, practice, practice.*

I know that getting experience sounds boring, but it's not. All you have to do is go out bird watching and remember to take your ears with you. Unless you're Vincent van Gogh, this should be easy to do.

✔ While in the field (or in your backyard), listen for bird sounds that you don't recognize.

✔ Choose a sound and try to locate its source.

✔ After you find the singer, listen to its song a few times and make mental notes about the song's pattern and quality.

While you're listening, watch the bird carefully; it may do something that cements the moment (and the bird's song) in your mind forever.

As you gain experience in birding by ear, you'll find yourself stopping whenever a strange call or song catches your attention. That's how it's supposed to happen! You'll find many interesting — even unexpected — birds if you use your ears in conjunction with your eyes.

Looking for singers

You hear a strange bird song, but you can't find the bird. What do you do?

Stop. Listen. Look.

That's the best way to find a singing bird. Each time the bird sings, try to figure out the direction from which the sound is coming. As you narrow the possibilities, try this trick:

Turn your head slightly from side to side, as if you're telling someone "no" in slow motion. Your ears will narrow down the directional possibilities as your head turns and the sound hits your eardrums from different angles.

If you have a good idea of the bird's direction, move slowly toward it, stopping to listen each time the bird sings. If you think you have the general location, scan it carefully for signs of movement. When you find the bird, watch to see whether it really is the one making the noise that you're following. Birds can put most human ventriloquists to shame.

If you're having trouble locating a singing bird, try cupping your hands behind your ears. This cupping helps to scoop the sounds into your ears more efficiently. It's a poor man's sound amplifier.

Helping your hearing

If you're even a little hard-of-hearing, you may have difficulty hearing high-pitched bird songs, such as warbler songs. Many bird watchers, especially men over the age of 50, naturally lose the high-end register of their hearing. This fact can be depressing to longtime birders who can *see* a male warbler singing but can't *hear* the song.

Some help is available for lost hearing, however. The help comes in the form of hearing aids adapted for use outdoors. These products were initially designed for use by hunters, but work equally well for bird watchers. In some cases, such as with a large group of birders, these hearing devices can amplify normal human conversation to painful volumes, but the fact remains that many a warbler song has been re-found with the help of modern hearing technology.

Consult a hearing specialist or an outdoor outfitter for brand names and ordering information.

Chapter 7

Bird Feeding: The Start of It All

Do you want to watch birds? Which birds are you going to watch? Are there any outside your window? No? Well, I have a suggestion: Why don't you try to attract some birds? It's as easy as rolling off a log, or pinching your finger in the car door. Just get some bird seed and place it in an easy-to-see spot outside your window. You can put the seed inside your window, but trust me, you'll get more birds (and fewer mice) if you put the seed outside.

There's No Place Like Home

The story is the same for feeding birds as it is for bird watching in general: start at home. Unless you live on the 999th floor of the Sears Tower in Chicago (or some similarly tall, hermetically sealed building), you, too, can enjoy luring unsuspecting birds in close, where you can ogle them to your heart's content. I start off with the *For Dummies*–approved, totally basic and foolproof method of feeding birds: Throw seed on the ground.

From the ground up

Believe it or not, starting a bird feeding station can be as simple as flinging a few handfuls of seed on the ground. I knew a dear old Connecticut Yankee who for 50 years did nothing more than this and had a devoted following of birds including fox sparrows, towhees, cardinals, chickadees, and a couple of titmice who learned her daily routine. They would peek into her bedroom, bathroom, or kitchen windows and tap on the glass if she was a little late in rising to throw a coffee can full of sunflower seed and table scraps out the back door!

There are a couple of messages in this little story. First, you really don't have to have expensive bird feeders to feed birds. Second, unexpected joys and surprises await you when you start feeding birds.

No takers

Sometimes people tell me, "I put up a bird feeder, but no birds will come to it." I never really understood why this would be so, until we moved to a rural area with heavy agriculture and very little tradition of bird feeding. I put up a bird feeder and nobody came! For weeks!

So I took a fresh look at bird feeders, from the point of view of a wild bird. Your typical tube feeder — all slippery plastic and shiny metal — is really a pretty scary thing to a naive wild bird. There's nothing natural about it, and even though you can see the seed inside it, a skittish bird may not want to land on it to figure out how to get at the seed.

So I dragged a hollow log out of the woods, sprinkled seed over it, and built a low, rough plywood and block table — nothing fancy — then stuck a bunch of dead branches into the ground around the whole setup. This gave birds some natural surfaces to land on and investigate. They came, they ate, they stayed — and they completely ignored the hanging tube feeder until the day a bold chickadee landed on it, scolding, and took the first sunflower seed. The other birds watched and learned, and I was on my way to having a great feeding station.

Think natural!

Sticks and stones. Think natural, and you'll be thinking like a bird.

Imagine yourself, a timorous little sparrow, skulking around the edge of the woods, scratching in the leaf litter for food. Would you fly across a big open green lawn, even if seed was on the ground? Wouldn't you be afraid of hawks and cats, dogs and people? Now, imagine a big, sheltering brushpile with lots of nooks and crannies to hide in smack dab in the middle of that feeding area. Sparrow heaven.

Lots of other birds will thank you by coming to your feeders if you build them a brushpile. We're not talking about something huge here, just a modest pile of sticks and brush, the kind of stuff you trim off your trees and shrubs on a Saturday afternoon, and then wonder what to do with. Toss it off to the side of your feeding station and watch the cardinals, sparrows, towhees, juncos, and chickadees pop in and out of it. You've given them a place to go when a hawk zooms by or the back door suddenly opens. It provides an out for the more skittish birds; they'll feel much freer to visit, knowing there's a place to hide nearby.

High or Low: Where Birds Feed

Feeding birds can take place in many ways. The two most basic methods are on the ground and from a suspended feeder. Most feeder operators do both to cater to the widest variety of birds, while some do only one or the other to discourage unwanted feeder visitors. Yes, some birds (and other critters) can become unwelcome at your feeding station. If you already feed birds, you probably know what I mean.

Beyond the basic ways to feed birds is the vast ocean of what to feed them.

Ground feeding

Ground feeding is great. Most of the bird species that come to feeders take all or part of their natural food from the ground anyway. In winter, though, there's snow and rain. That can spoil seed that's scattered on the ground, and spoiled seed can lead to sick birds. To avoid this, clever humans have come up with a variety of feeders that either keep the seed up off the ground, keep it dry by dispensing a little at a time, or both. The most basic bird feeder is a low table, called a platform feeder (see Figure 7-1).

Figure 7-1: A pair of California quail, a green-tailed towhee, and a plain titmouse visit a platform feeder.

These feeders are easy to make with a couple of cinder blocks and a sheet of plywood. If you want to get fancy, you can tack some quarter-round around the edges to help contain the seed, and drill ½-inch drain holes in the plywood. Bird tables are a nice, non-threatening way to keep seed up off the ground but are still accessible to ground-feeding birds like juncos, sparrows, towhees, doves, and cardinals. Big flocks of birds can feed without the jostling and bickering engendered by tube or hanging feeders. Make sure to clean your platform feeder frequently.

A slightly different version of this simple bird table replaces the plywood bottom with screen. It's best to go for stainless steel screen, with a fairly coarse mesh. This lets water drain right through the seed, and lets air get to it to dry it out. It still gets clogged up, of course, but a knock on the ground or blast with the hose will clear it right out. Several commercial screen-bottomed feeding platforms are out there, or you can make your own.

The drawback to ground feeding is that the seed is exposed to the weather so it gets soaked by rain and covered up by snow and ice, and so on. There's the additional problem of hygiene: Birds feeding on the ground don't politely fly away when they need to relieve themselves, so the food can get contaminated. The answer is to offer food in raised or hanging feeders.

Suspended or raised feeders

Birds that find their food in bushes, trees, and in other off-the-ground places prefer to feed at bird feeders that are elevated. These are the stereotypical bird feeders that hang from a tree branch, deck railing, or window frame. You can find many variations on the design of hanging feeders.

Hundreds of types and styles of bird feeders exist. If you're just starting out in bird feeding, I recommend that you keep things simple. Get one or two simple feeders and feed one or two seed types, until you get a feel for whether you and the birds are enjoying this new adventure. Don't make the mistake of going whole hog with 12 new feeders and a half-ton of seed. You'll be worn out from just filling the feeders!

Buying Feeders

Let's talk about commercially available feeders. These shiny, clanky things have a lot going for them. First and foremost, they keep the seed fresh and dry. It can be snowing like mad, covering up your bird table and ground feeding area in seconds, and a good hanging feeder will still be calmly dispensing seed to the hungry.

Feeder types

Commercial feeders come in three basic types: hopper, tube, and satellite.

Hoppers (not Dennis)

Hopper feeders have a lot of different styles, but the old favorite looks like a little barn or covered bridge, minus the young lovers and graffiti. The sides are usually panels of Plexiglas that allow you to see how much seed remains, and access is usually through the top.

A good hopper feeder can be completely disassembled to be cleaned (more on this later). Hoppers can be pole-mounted, often with a threaded sleeve that screws onto the threaded top of a plumber's galvanized pipe. They can be suspended, too.

The two best features of hoppers are

- They hold a lot of seed, so that you don't have to go out every day to refill them.

- They're big and bird-friendly. Shy birds, or big birds like doves and jays and woodpeckers, are able to land and feed from them comfortably.

When I've had unusual species such as rose-breasted gros-beaks at my feeder, they've come to hopper feeders. Birds that are reluctant to perch on tube feeders or cling to satellite feeders will happily come to a hopper feeder.

You can feed any kind of seed in a hopper feeder because the seed usually comes out of slots at the bottom of the Plexiglas panels. Sunflower seed is a favorite of many hopper feeder visitors, but seed mixes containing millet, corn, and peanut hearts can be fed in these feeders, too.

Totally tubular

Tube feeders — long cylinders with perches at the feeding ports — are the classic feeders for woodland birds like chick-adees, titmice, woodpeckers, and nuthatches, as well as for finches like goldfinches, siskins, and house finches. All these birds are small, and they can perch comfortably on the usually short metal perches most tube feeders have (see Figure 7-2).

Figure 7-2: Small, seed-eating birds such as finches and chickadees like tube feeders.

Tube feeders are great for screening out big birds like blue jays, grackles, blackbirds, and doves, if you're into avian discrimination. But they also keep grosbeaks and cardinals away, too, because these birds aren't so good at clinging, and they're just too big for the perches. They'll go to the hopper or platform feeders, or onto the ground. When you're looking at tube feeders, make sure the seed you're planning to put in them will fit through the holes at the feeding ports. Most have big holes that let sunflower seed through, but others are made especially for the tiny thistle or niger seed.

What to look for when buying

Many feeder styles are on the market, but any feeder you buy should be easily filled, emptied, and cleaned.

> ✔ Beware of feeders that require you to use a funnel to fill them because you'll quickly tire of lugging a funnel out every time you have to replenish the seed.

✔ Wooden parts of hopper feeders should be made of weather-resistant cedar, or stained or painted to protect against moisture. Plastic feeders should be reinforced with metal around the feeding ports to ward off chewing squirrels. Perches should be metal or replaceable dowel, for the same squirrelly reasons. Because you may be looking at a feeder for a decade or more, it pays to buy the sturdiest and most easily maintained one you can.

✔ With tube feeders, look at the bottom port. Is there dead space beneath it where seed can collect because the birds can't reach it? This seed gets all icky and moldy — a waste of food, and dangerous for the birds.

✔ Can you take the feeder apart to scrub and clean it? If it looks like you'll need fancy bottle brushes or an act of Congress to get it clean, pick one of simpler design.

✔ Beware of super-cheap feeders. Not all of the $5 to $10 feeders available for sale are going to last you for more than one season of feeding. Remember, these things are going to be filled with seed and hung out in the weather. Look for durable construction if you want to get your money's worth.

The ideal feeding station

By now, a picture should be emerging of an ideal feeding station — one with a variety of different feeder styles, at different heights, where the greatest diversity of birds can find food. It should provide shelter from wind, rain, and predators in the form of shrubbery or the instant habitat of brushpiles and found materials. It should have a wide variety of foods, and some water should be available year-round.

Feeding Times: When to Start, When to Stop

The vast majority of people feed birds only in winter, when it's truly tough out there and the birds look so pitiful all puffed up against the cold. But feeding birds year-round has lots of benefits. It's up to you when you want to feed.

If you do want to feed in the winter, start feeding in autumn before the weather turns really nasty. This way, you'll entice birds into including your feeder in their winter feeding routes. Think of the flocks using your feeder as an ever-changing river of birds and you'll have a good idea how it works. You may think you have the same five chickadees all day long, but it's more likely that you have 30 or 40 chickadees who stop in for a few minutes every day, and then go on their merry way looking for caterpillar cocoons, scale insects, and spiders hiding under tree bark. So the sooner in autumn you have the station going, the more birds you're likely to snag.

The birds give you clues

The birds tell you when you can stop feeding in the spring. Long after the grass has greened up, you'll still have lots of birds at your feeder. Even after the weather has warmed up, nights can still drop below freezing, which keeps the insects inactive. But one fine April or May day, as the leaves are unfurling, it occurs to you that the feeders just aren't emptying as fast as usual, and you aren't going out quite as often to fill them. In our yard, this is quite dramatic, because we have a flock of about 250 American goldfinches who pig-out at the feeders all winter. By late April, the males have shed their dull winter plumage for brilliant yellow, trimmed with black wings, cap and tail. They're singing like crazy in every treetop; it can be deafening. And all of a sudden, they leave, dispersing to the surrounding countryside to pair up and eventually breed. It's quiet. And by then, I really don't miss them at all!

Migratory birds follow their instincts

Birds are happy to desert your feeders when it's time to migrate, or when protein-rich insects become available. You don't need to worry about getting them addicted to seed, or keeping them from their normal migratory behavior. But this leads to another question.

Suppose that Aunt Reba just called. The condo in Florida is free for ten days. You take a look at the 20-pound icicles hanging from the eaves and say, yes. Only as you're locking the door behind you does it occur to you — who's going to feed the birds? Will they die without the handouts they've grown accustomed to?

There's no really clear-cut answer to this because a lot depends on whether other feeding stations are nearby. Studies have shown that chickadees take, on average, only one-quarter of their daily food from feeders. Flocking species, like goldfinches, siskins, and house finches, though, seem more inclined to camp out at feeders, relying more heavily on them for their daily meals. Birds are intelligent and resourceful enough to move elsewhere when a food source is exhausted.

Resident birds need continuity

Some bird species keep winter territories from which they don't wander. Cardinals and white-throated sparrows are two examples. For them, a stop-and-start feeding program can be worse than none at all.

When you have a successful feeding station, populations of birds can explode. And even though the birds may be taking most of their food from your feeders, the natural food supply in the immediate vicinity of the feeders is bound to be exhausted soon. There's not much for the birds to fall back on should the feeding stop. Pulling the rug out from under territorial species who live right around your yard is unfair, at best.

If you're going away for only a couple of days, fill all your feeders, and scatter a lot of seed on the ground and under shrubbery. For longer vacations, we pay a neighbor to fill our feeders while watering our plants and feeding our indoor pets. We look at it as having a few hundred outdoor pets.

Maintaining Your Feeder Station

Okay now, let me talk about hygiene. It makes me feel better.

When you feed several hundred individual birds, as we do at our rural feeding station, things can get whitewashed in a hurry, and it's not nice — for the birds or for their poor human servants who have to refill the feeders.

Keep cleaning stuff handy

I keep a pair of rubber boots by the front door that I wear only to fill the feeders, so that I don't track all that stuff through the house. At the feeding station, I keep an old spatula, a couple of chopsticks, and a scrub brush. The spatula is great for clearing away seed hulls on table and hopper feeders. The chopsticks can quickly ream out drainage holes or get at gunk stuck below feeding ports in tube feeders. The scrub brush, with a bucket of hot water, takes care of that sickly sweet-smelling sunflower guck that accumulates in wet weather. It's made up of bits of uneaten sunflower meats, hulls, and goodness knows what else. Phew.

When I'm truly in a Teutonic frenzy, I get out the Clorox and make a solution of one part bleach to nine parts hot water. I soak the feeders in this, scrub them out, douse the platforms and scrub them . . . just do a good number on the whole feeding station.

Clean up for healthy birds

There are good reasons other than one's personal hygienic orientation to keep your feeders well-cleaned. Disease. Yup. You can do a whole lot of good by feeding birds. But you can also do harm by inviting so many guests to one table because, unlike most human dinner guests over two years of age, birds poop while they eat. Being birds, they don't pay a whole lot of attention to where, either. It's not something birds have to deal with when they're flying around free, but when you get a couple hundred birds in maybe 20 square feet, you have a poopfest. And along with this goes the potential for spreading disease in your feeder flock.

Watch where the food falls

To get around this problem, you can start by keeping your ground feeding out from under the hanging feeders and perches. I usually throw the seed in a wide circle outside the immediate feeder area, and I keep changing the place I throw it. Enough seed will fall out of the feeders that you'll always have birds directly under the feeders, too. Remember that brushpile? Not only do we burn it in May, but we also change the brush a few times each winter. If the feeding area gets really disgusting, we move it, lock, stock, and barrel, to a different part of the yard.

When we first started feeding, we hung the feeders right off our deck. Hoo, boy. The flocks sat up on our television antenna in between meals and made a real mess of our deck. If you're into hosing and scrubbing a lot, feeding birds over your deck may be an option, but it's better to hang the feeders over grass, where you won't be walking.

 Here's an idea that may work for you. Because the grass under heavily used feeders takes a beating, try spreading bark mulch under your feeders. When it gets full of hulls and droppings, rake it up, compost it, and spread a fresh layer of mulch.

Bird Seed Types

Just like people, birds eat just about anything they can digest. And just like people, all birds have certain food types that they prefer enormously over others. The good news for you is that people have been feeding birds for many decades, so that you get the benefit of all that trial-and-error experimentation. These days, we, the bird-feeding public, already know what foods birds prefer. At the feeders this means seeds.

But which seeds are the best?

Table 7-1 provides the general food preferences for the most common feeder birds of North America. Foods are listed in approximate order of preference.

Table 7-1	Bird Food Preference Chart
Species	*Preferred Foods*
Quail, pheasants	Cracked corn, millet, wheat, milo
Pigeons, doves	Millet, cracked corn, wheat, milo, niger, buckwheat, sunflower, baked goods
Roadrunner	Meat scraps, hamburger, suet

Species	Preferred Foods
Hummingbirds	Plant nectar, small insects, sugar solution
Woodpeckers	Suet, meat scraps, sunflower hearts/seed, cracked corn, peanuts, fruits, sugar solution
Jays	Peanuts, sunflower, suet, meat scraps, cracked corn, baked goods, mealworms
Crows, magpies, and nutcracker	Meat scraps, suet, cracked corn, peanuts, baked goods, leftovers, dog food, mealworms
Titmice, chickadees	Peanut kernels, sunflower, suet, peanut butter
Nuthatches	Suet, suet mixes, sunflower hearts and seed, peanut kernels, peanut butter, mealworms
Wrens, creepers	Suet, suet mixes, peanut butter, peanut kernels, bread, fruit, millet (wrens), mealworms
Mockingbirds, thrashers, catbirds	Halved apple, chopped fruits, baked goods, suet, nutmeats, millet (thrashers), soaked raisins, currants, sunflower hearts
Robins, bluebirds, other thrushes	Suet, suet mixes, mealworms, berries, baked goods, chopped fruits, soaked raisins, currants, nutmeats, sunflower hearts
Kinglets	Suet, suet mixes, baked goods, mealworms
Waxwings	Berries, chopped fruits, canned peas, currants, raisins, suet dough, mealworms
Warblers	Suet, suet mixes, fruit, baked goods, sugar solution, chopped nutmeats, mealworms
Tanagers	Suet, fruits, sugar solution, mealworms, baked goods
Cardinals, grosbeaks, pyrrhuloxias (a type of cardinal)	Sunflower, safflower, cracked corn, millet, fruit, suet dough, mealworms
Towhees, juncos	Millet, sunflower, cracked corn, peanuts, baked goods, nutmeats, mealworms
Sparrows, buntings	Millet, sunflower hearts, black-oil sunflower, cracked corn, baked goods, mealworms

(continued)

Table 7-1 *(continued)*

Species	Preferred Foods
Blackbirds, starlings	Cracked corn, milo, wheat, table scraps, baked goods, suet, mealworms
Orioles	Halved oranges, apples, berries, sugar solution, grape jelly, suet, suet mixes, soaked raisins, mealworms and currants
Finches, siskins	Thistle (niger), sunflower hearts, black-oil sunflower seed, millet, canary seed, fruits, peanut kernels, suet mixes

In a nutshell, sunflower seed is the best. So if you're just starting out in feeding, I suggest you buy some black-oil sunflower seed at a local hardware store, feed store, specialty bird store, or even at a major retail chain store. But you need to watch out for certain things when buying seed. The following sections describe the best kinds of seed, in descending order of popularity.

Black-oil sunflower

Smaller than gray-striped sunflower seed, with a thin, all-black, papery shell, black-oil sunflower seed can be cracked by sparrows, juncos, and even small-billed goldfinches. It's a better buy, too, because 70 percent of each seed is meat, compared to only 57 percent for striped sunflower. Its high oil and fat content helps birds get through cold winter nights. Black-oil sunflower seed is the heart of any feeding program because it's the seed accepted by the greatest variety of birds. You can feed it out of hanging feeders, put it in hoppers or on tables, or scatter it on the ground — preferably all of the above.

Have a sunflower heart

If I were to pick only one food to offer at my feeding station, it would be sunflower hearts. Yes, they're expensive, but a bag of sunflower hearts (no shells, just the meat of the seed) lasts more than three times as long as a bag of seeds with shells. Not only this, but every species that comes to my feeding station eats them. Being hull-less, hearts are accessible to weaker billed birds like siskins, redpolls, and Carolina wrens. Goldfinches love them.

Keep dry

Compared to seeds with hulls, hearts are relatively free of waste and of the messy shells that pile up to smother grass and rot decks. The only drawback is that the hearts shouldn't be exposed to wet weather; thus, they should be fed only from feeders. They rot quickly when damp. On dry days, it's fine to spread a handful on the bird table, but otherwise, stick to weatherproof feeders. You'll be surprised how little it takes to feed a lot of birds.

Getting a good mix

Mixed seed, often generically referred to as "wild bird seed," is a vital addition to any feeding program. Not all mixes are created equal, however, and what is eagerly eaten in Arizona can go to waste in New York. A prime example is milo, a round, reddish seed that looks like a BB. You'll see it, along with wheat, oats, and even barley, in the grocery-store mixes mentioned next in this chapter. In the East, milo and wheat are spurned by most birds except blackbirds and doves. In the West, however, quail, doves, towhees, and sparrows eagerly eat milo.

Millet

Despite certain regional preferences, birds everywhere will eat some foods. Go for a mix that consists primarily of white proso millet, a little, round, shiny, cream-colored seed. It's a staple for most sparrows and juncos, and birds as diverse as doves, Carolina wrens, thrashers, and cardinals will eat it, too.

Cracked corn

The second foolproof ingredient of a mix is cracked corn, which is accepted by most birds after the sunflower and millet is gone. Cracked corn is the cheapest and best offering for quail, pheasants, and doves, but it's irresistible to blackbirds, cowbirds, grackles, and house sparrows. If you're inundated by these less-desirable birds, you may want to pull in your corn horns.

Sunflower seed and peanut hearts

The third ingredient of a good mix is our old buddy, black-oil sunflower seed. Peanut hearts, which are small, rather bitter byproducts of peanut processing, make bird seed mixes smell good (which is nice for us), boost the price (which is nice for retailers), and may appeal to chickadees, titmice, jays, and wrens. Peanut hearts are not vital and, in my experience, the sunflower always goes first anyway. This isn't to devalue whole peanuts as a food — they can be great if offered in the right feeder.

Other options: Thistle and safflower

A couple of the more obscure seeds have their adherents.

Niger, or **thistle seed,** is imported from Africa and Asia. The seed is sterilized, so it won't germinate and take over back-yards all over North America. Lots of people are under the misapprehension that thistle seed is the only thing American goldfinches eat. I have a couple of hundred goldfinches here who would faint if I served them this expensive little treat; they do just fine on black-oil sunflower.

In addition to being expensive, niger is subject to mold, especially in hot, damp weather, and you have to shake your feeders every time you fill them to be sure the seed is coming out of the ports properly. If the seed clumps, you may have to dump it out where the birds won't find it, and wash and dry your feeder before refilling it. Fine mesh "thistle socks" are a cheap way to feed niger, and they let air circulate around the seed. I hear from a lot of people about batches of niger that the birds just won't eat; it looks fine, smells fine, but probably tastes bad. All in all, sunflower is a better all-around choice.

Safflower is a white, shiny, conical seed that's gaining popularity among people who find that cardinals like it, and some squirrels and grackles don't. The operative word in that statement is some. Lots of squirrels love safflower seed. You may want to try it and see. Safflower seed is usually found in bulk at better feed stores. You can offer it in any feeder that dispenses sunflower seed, or scatter it on the ground to attract cardinals (who aren't much for perching on tube feeders). Once again, safflower seed is nice to offer, but not vital; any bird that eats safflower will also take sunflower seed.

Other Bird Foods

You can offer birds a vast array of other foods besides bird seed. Here are a few of the most commonly offered parts of the birds' smorgasbord.

Peanuts

Peanuts are a vital part of my feeding program. Offered in the shell, only crows, jays, and the occasional clever titmouse can really exploit them, because peanuts are just too big and cumbersome for most birds to crack open. Better feed and birdseed stores, though, sell raw, shelled peanuts in bulk. Because I can't always find these in my area, I buy the cheapest, unsalted, roasted cocktail peanuts (sold in jars).

Offer these peanuts in a feeder that keeps larger birds from carrying them away whole. You can use a sturdy nylon mesh onion bag to hold them and hang it from a wire, or you can easily make your own peanut feeder out of ¼-inch mesh hardware cloth. Roll the mesh hardware cloth into a cylinder, crimp the bottom shut, cut and fold over a flap for the top, secure it with a piece of wire, and hang it where squirrels can't reach it. And make sure that you don't leave any sharp wires protruding that may injure a bird.

The idea is to allow birds to peck small bits out of the peanuts, not carry whole nuts off. Peanuts offer a great, high-protein boost to winter-weary birds, and help insect-eaters like wrens, woodpeckers, and sometimes even sapsuckers make it through.

Peanuts can be subject to mold in hot, wet weather. Check them often for signs of black mold or the darkening in color that can mean they've gone rancid. Offer only as many as the birds will eat in a few days in warmer weather conditions, doling them out like the gold they are.

Peanut butter: The universal bait

If you offer peanut butter, but the woodpeckers, chickadees, and titmice will love you for it. You can make a simple peanut butter feeder by drilling shallow one-inch holes in a piece of scrap wood, filling them with peanut butter, and hanging it up near your feeders.

Gouge out a few toeholds underneath each hole to help the birds cling. If the food goes unrecognized, try sticking a few sunflower seeds in the peanut butter — the birds soon get the idea and come back for more. Now you know what to do with those jars of PB in the back of the cabinet, the ones that are just a little too old to devote to toast or late-night snacking. Soon, you may be buying the cheapest store brands you can find to keep up with the feathered fans.

Suet is fat city

Suet is the dense, white fat that collects around beef kidneys and loins. You'll find it in most grocery store meat counters, sometimes rolled into balls with mixed birdseed on the outside. Avoid this, and just buy it by the chunk; it's cheaper.

You'll be surprised at how many different species eat suet, including some you may need to look up in the field guide. All the regular seed-eaters — chickadees, titmice, nuthatches, woodpeckers — eat suet, as well as wrens, sapsuckers, warblers, orioles, catbirds, creepers, and other birds. A little suet goes a long way.

Keep a couple of things in mind about suet, though. Be sure not to mistake the inedible white "rind" left when all the fat is pecked away for edible suet. And in warm weather, put very small pieces out, as it liquefies and turns rancid after a few days in the hot sun.

Avoid suet spoilage

Suet left out in the hot sun turns into rancid suet. If you smell it once, you'll never let it get that gross again. And think about the poor birds! With little or no sense of smell to warn them away! There oughta be a law! Rancid suet is no good for birds, and may make them sick.

If you feel you must offer suet all summer, consider doing one of these things:

- ✔ Offer suet in a cool, shaded location. Monitor the suet so if it does go bad, you can remove it.

- ✔ Bring your suet inside during the hot part of the day.

- ✔ Offer one of the commercially available, rendered-suet cakes. Rendered suet doesn't melt so readily.

Render or not

Lots of people like to render suet. They say rendered suet keeps better and is easier to handle because the suet is harder, once it sets up. They melt the suet in the microwave. Then, while the suet is still liquid, they add special ingredients like peanut butter, cornmeal, flour, or chopped peanuts and sunflower hearts. Then they refrigerate or freeze the suet in blocks that fit easily into the commercial suet feeders.

Render the suet outside, if render you must! I tried rendering suet inside in an electric frypan once. Before we moved it outside on the deck, it made the house smell like a cheap diner, it took a long time to make, and then I had a greasy skillet to wash. I went back to offering the raw, unrendered fat, and the birds didn't miss a beat.

Buy suet blocks

Lots of people take convenience a step further and buy commercial suet blocks. Some of these blocks are great; some aren't so great.

Avoid commercial blocks that have whole seed, like sunflower and millet seed, melted into them. These blocks are difficult for birds to use because they can't crack the fat-soaked shells, and they wind up just picking the seeds out of the suet and discarding them.

If you buy blocks, buy those with 100-percent-edible ingredients like peanut hearts, sunflower hearts, chopped raisins, or cornmeal.

In my experience, the fuss of rendering suet, or the expense of buying blocks, isn't justified by any greater enthusiasm on the part of the birds who eat it. They're just as happy with the meat-counter lumps. But do offer suet as part of your feeding program, and you'll be rewarded by lots of interesting woodpecker behavior. Woodpeckers will gladly visit suet feeders year-round. We have whole families of downy, red-bellied, and even hairy woodpeckers all summer and winter. They're just as glad not to have to peck out a living all the time. Think about it: If you had a choice between having chili served in a bowl or having to open the can with your teeth, wouldn't you pick the bowl?

Fruit-full results

When I noticed yellow-bellied sapsuckers, robins, and pileated woodpeckers eating the last shriveled apples and pears in our orchard, I began offering halved apples, impaled on short twigs of the dead branches we put up all around our feeder. Red apples were eaten by red-bellied woodpeckers, sapsuckers, house finches, robins, and starlings, while green ones went untouched. I'm not sure why the birds had this preference. Where's Dr. Know-It-All when you really need him? Or her?

Other fruits you can offer in winter include raisins and currants. These fruits need to be chopped up and soaked in hot water to soften them. Mockingbirds, catbirds, wrens, and thrashers appreciate these most, although bluebirds and other thrushes sometimes take them, too.

Save halved oranges and fruits such as cherries, peaches, bananas, and berries for spring and summer, when the orioles and tanagers that prefer them are back from the tropics.

Chapter 8

Ten Bird Myths

● ●

In This Chapter

▶ Debunking age-old bird myths

▶ Sage advice on handling misinformation

▶ Amazing feats of verbiage

● ●

*J*ust about the time you're ready to consider yourself an intermediate bird watcher, along come people who aren't bird watchers making wildly inaccurate and sweeping statements about birds, and looking to you to confirm their facts — or challenge their accuracy.

This situation puts you in the somewhat squirmy position of having to be an expert on birds. That's human nature: Anyone who knows more about a certain subject than you do must be an expert — and, in this case, you're the expert.

To help you prepare for your transformation into a bird expert, here's my list of "The Top Ten Great Bird Myths" people believe about birds, along with the facts — and nothing but the facts.

May the farce be with you.

Hummingbirds Migrate on the Backs of Geese

How this got started I may never know. But it is one of the most fervently believed myths about birds and nature there is. Perhaps when Elvis comes out of hiding he can set us straight on the subject. Although it seems logical for hummingbirds to hitch a ride, in reality they have to make it through spring and fall migration on their own two wings.

Take Down the Feeders So the Hummingbirds Will Migrate

Hey, the hummers leave when the geese do. Those Vs of geese in the sky are actually pointing out for hummingbirds the direction of the nearest hummingbird feeder.

Seriously, though, hummingbirds know instinctively when to migrate. Nothing you do short of capturing them (which is illegal) can keep them longer than they want to stay.

Birds Will Starve If We Stop Feeding

This isn't really true. Yes, feeding stations may help more birds survive during extremely harsh winter weather, but birds don't rely exclusively on your feeders for their sustenance. Birds have wings and tend to use them. If food is within flying distance, most birds can survive just fine.

A Baby Bird on the Ground Has Always Fallen from the Nest

Many ground-dwelling species have young that can survive very well on the ground, even before they're able to fly. Killdeer, quail, turkeys, and ducks are among the species that have young that survive for long periods on the ground.

The best thing to do if you find a baby bird on the ground is to leave it where it is. A parent may be taking care of it. Even if you don't see an adult bird nearby, chances are that the parents are near and the nestling will be fine. Most baby birds leave the nest before they can fly very well, so the occasional landing on the ground is perfectly normal. If you're certain the bird has fallen from the nest, but you cannot locate the nest or can't return the bird to it, call a licensed bird rehabilitator for help. It is illegal to handle or possess native wild birds. You must have a special permit to do so.

Don't Touch a Baby Bird Because the Mother Will Smell Your Scent and Abandon It

Touching or handling a baby bird is never a good idea. But if you do handle a baby bird, you won't doom the youngster to abandonment because birds have almost no sense of smell. Predatory mammals, on the other hand, can smell quite well. What you might be doing by handling a baby bird, or by peering into an active bird nest you have discovered, is laying down a scent path for a hungry raccoon, opossum, skunk, or fox. These mammals know that human scent often means an easy meal. Think about it: dog dishes, compost piles, garbage cans, picnic areas, and dumpsters behind fast-food restaurants — these human-scented items and places are all positive associations for a hungry mammal.

For this reason I always avoid bird nests, and I try never to touch nestlings or eggs.

Robins Are Always a Sign of Spring

In some areas of North America, robins probably are a sign of spring. But robins don't migrate away from cold weather in all areas. They do change their behavior from lawn-hopping earthworm hunters to woodland-dwelling berry eaters.

Some better signs of spring are the first *peent*ing woodcock, the first hummingbird at the garden flowers, or the first bird fighting its reflection in your kitchen window.

Each Spring, the Swallows Return Faithfully to Capistrano

Most of the swallows in San Juan de Capistrano, California, are cliff swallows and are mostly resident birds, which means that they don't all go away in the winter. Because they never leave, they cannot return. But it's a great story just the same.

The Bald Eagle Is a Fierce Predator

In reality, bald eagles are turkey vultures with a press agent. Bald eagles, the symbol of the United States, are more scavengers than fierce killers. They would much rather swoop down to feed on a dead fish than get all wet trying to actually catch one. When they hunt, they do a good job of it.

Bald eagles aren't really bald, either. Am I bursting your bubble?

John James Audubon Is the Father of American Bird Protection

In reality, Audubon shot birds left and right. In his day, before binoculars, bird watching was done over the sights of a gun. Birds were killed and then carefully examined in the hand. At least Audubon ate most of the birds he killed, and reported in his journals on the relative taste of all of the species on which he dined.

All Vultures Are "Buzzards"; All Gulls Are "Seagulls"

Buzzards are actually European *Buteo* hawks, related to our red-tailed and rough-legged hawks. This term is in common use in Europe, but for some reason is improperly used by non-bird watchers in North America to refer to North American vultures.

Many of our North American gulls live their lives out with only an occasional glimpse of the sea. Although some species are closely associated with salt water, two species that nest well-inland are the Franklin's gull and ring-billed gull. We have Richard Bach's *Jonathan Livingston Seagull* to thank for cementing that one in popular culture.

Index

Most binoculars are designed for the "average man." Finally, one that fits the average *person*.

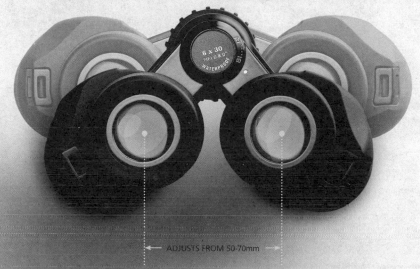

← ADJUSTS FROM 50-70mm →

INTRODUCING NEW LEUPOLD® YOSEMITE SERIES 6X30MM BINOCULARS, the ideal binocular for anyone in your family. Most full-size binoculars were designed for adult men, and have a minimum interpupillary distance that's too wide for users with smaller faces. Only Leupold Yosemites adjust from 50mm to 70mm, so they'll fit everyone from children to adults. The 6x magnification and wide field of view make Yosemites especially easy to use when locating birds or other wildlife. They're also lightweight and designed to fit perfectly in smaller hands. With a multi-coated lens system for brightness and clarity, long eye relief, and rugged, waterproof construction, new Leupold Yosemites put serious optical power within anyone's reach. For the Leupold Dealer nearest you, call 1-800-929-4949, or visit our Web site at www.leupold.com.

DURABLE, RUBBER ARMOR COATING — AVAILABLE IN BLACK, NATURAL OR RED, THE YOSEMITES ARE JUST AS AT HOME IN THE WOODS, AT A GAME, OR ANYWHERE YOU NEED SERIOUS OUTDOOR OPTICS.

LEUPOLD®
AMERICA'S OPTICS AUTHORITY®

© 2006 Leupold & Stevens, Inc.

HEALTH & SELF-HELP

0-7645-6820-5 *†   0-7645-2566-2

Also available:
- Alzheimer's For Dummies
  0-7645-3899-3
- Asthma For Dummies
  0-7645-4233-8
- Controlling Cholesterol For
  Dummies
  0-7645-5440-9
- Depression For Dummies
  0-7645-3900-0
- Dieting For Dummies
  0-7645-4149-8
- Fertility For Dummies
  0-7645-2549-2

- Fibromyalgia For Dummies
  0-7645-5441-7
- Improving Your Memory
  For Dummies
  0-7645-5435-2
- Pregnancy For Dummies †
  0-7645-4483-7
- Quitting Smoking For Dummies
  0-7645-2629-4
- Relationships For Dummies
  0-7645-5384-4
- Thyroid For Dummies
  0-7645-5385-2

EDUCATION, HISTORY, REFERENCE & TEST PREPARATION

0-7645-5194-9   0-7645-4186-2

Also available:
- Algebra For Dummies
  0-7645-5325-9
- British History For Dummies
  0-7645-7021-8
- Calculus For Dummies
  0-7645-2498-4
- English Grammar For Dummies
  0-7645-5322-4
- Forensics For Dummies
  0-7645-5580-4
- The GMAT for Dummies
  0-7645-5251-1
- Inglés Para Dummies
  0-7645-5427-1

- Italian For Dummies
  0-7645-5196-5
- Latin For Dummies
  0-7645-5431-X
- Lewis & Clark For Dummies
  0-7645-2545-X
- Research Papers For Dummies
  0-7645-5426-3
- The SAT I For Dummies
  0-7645-7193-1
- Science Fair Projects For Dummies
  0-7645-5460-3
- U.S. History For Dummies
  0-7645-5249-X

Get smart @ dummies.com®

- Find a full list of Dummies titles
- Look into loads of FREE on-site articles
- Sign up for FREE eTips e-mailed to you weekly
- See what other products carry the Dummies name
- Shop directly from the Dummies bookstore
- Enter to win new prizes every month!